WORLD-CLASS
LEADERSHIP
Leading Yourself, Your Team,
The World and Society

WORLD-CLASS LEADERSHIP

Leading Yourself,
Your Team,
The World and
Society

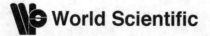

Tetsuya Abe | EQ Partners,Inc., Japan
Sachin Chowdhery | Change Co., Ltd., Japan
Abacus Venture Solutions Pvt. Ltd., India

World Scientific

NEW JERSEY · LONDON · SINGAPORE · BEIJING · SHANGHAI · HONG KONG · TAIPEI · CHENNAI

Published by

World Scientific Publishing Co. Pte. Ltd.

5 Toh Tuck Link, Singapore 596224

USA office: 27 Warren Street, Suite 401-402, Hackensack, NJ 07601

UK office: 57 Shelton Street, Covent Garden, London WC2H 9HE

British Library Cataloguing-in-Publication Data
A catalogue record for this book is available from the British Library.

WORLD-CLASS LEADERSHIP
Leading Yourself, Your Team, The World and Society

ISBN-13 978-981-4360-71-5
ISBN-10 981-4360-71-6

In-house Editor: Sandhya Venkatesh

Typeset by Stallion Press
Email: enquiries@stallionpress.com

Printed in Singapore.

PREFACE

Since the later part of the 20th century, especially after 1990 till now, the world has been experiencing great changes. Some representative examples include the world financial crisis that arose due to subprime problems in the United States in 2007 and the Lehman shock in 2008, and the world economic crisis soon after. It can be said that we are experiencing a period of rapid change.

Some may experience the change strongly, some moderately, and some of us may not feel the change at all. However, there is no doubt that the world has been undergoing drastic change.

Changes in the world and the business environment inevitably mean that the approach to leadership needs to be changed accordingly.

Leadership styles have been studied extensively for more than 2000 years — since the times of the Greeks and the Romans, and China's Confucius period. Though leadership styles have changed to some extent, there are few elements which remain unchanged.

Since the late 20th century until now, three developments have affected the form and function of leadership significantly. They are internetization, economic globalization, and diversification.

The world has been changing, and so have leadership styles. Leadership styles that were adopted previously can no longer be applied to good effect in this changing environment.

It is important to transform the leadership approach according to the changing environment, to exercise effective leadership.

The business environment in the 21st century has changed beyond imagination. These changes are akin to the tip of an iceberg. We can foresee many more changes in the coming years.

Leadership in the 21st century is more difficult and complicated, and requires swift actions. They purpose of this book is to summarize the common elements of leadership for the new era, so that many people can understand and put these into practice.

I have attended lectures by several great business managers and leaders in Japan and overseas, and have had dialogues with them. Some of them include. Fujio Cho (former president of Toyota), Katsuaki Watanabe (former president of Toyota), Carlos Ghosn (CEO of Nissan and Renault), Takeo Fukui (president of Honda), Kunio Nakamura (former CEO of Matsushita Electric Industrial or Panasonic, as we know it today), Fumio Ohtsubo (president of Matsushita–Panasonic), Atsutoshi Nishida (former president of Toshiba), Toshifumi Suzuki (Chairman/CEO of Seven & i Holdings), Masayoshi Son (president of Softbank), Yoshiharu Hoshino (president of Hoshino Resort) from Japan, and Jack Welch (former CEO of General Electric), Louis Gerstner (former CEO of IBM), Rudy Giuliani (former Governor of New York), Narayana Murthy (chairman of Infosys), and Jack Ma (CEO of Alibaba) from around the world.

I have also lectured and held discussions on several aspects of leadership with over 2000 people per year in companies such as NEC, Toshiba, Fuji Film, Casio, Canon, Kao, Sumitomo Corporation, Mizuho Group, and Yellow Hat. My understanding has deepened further through my interactions with colleagues and students at Rikkyo University, Japan.

For the past five years, I have been attending training sessions at the American Society for Training & Development (ASTD) — one of the world's leading associations for human resource development — on the latest world trends in leadership development. I have also attended a leadership course conducted by Massachusetts Institute of Technology's Peter Senge, who is an authority on the subject.

In this book, I have summarized everything I learnt from my discussions with executives and workers of many companies, university researchers, and students. The book is written in a simple and accessible manner and the information provided can be put in practice as needed.

It is my sincere hope that everyone who is interested in developing leadership in the new era, including the readers of this book may learn from each other, to develop and grow in the future.

Lastly, I would like to thank you for your interest in this book. I will be very glad if this book can be of use in your business or any other activity while contributing to your well-being.

Now, let us begin our journey toward world-class leadership that will lead in the 21st century.

Tetsuya ABE
Representative Director/MBA, EQ Partners, Inc.
Part-time Lecturer: Graduate School of Rikkyo University
admin@eqpartners.com
August 2010

CONTENTS

ACKNOWLEDGMENTS

I would like to express my gratitude to the people who were involved in my business, university and social activities and learning sessions in the course of publishing this book. I would especially like to express my heartfelt gratitude and appreciation to the following people:

My former bosses, senior associates, co-workers, junior staff members, and various business partners who have given me advice in the 16 years of my business experience at Matsushita Electric Industry (Panasonic).

Business associates from various companies, including Toshiba Group, NEC Group, Fuji Film, Sumitomo Corporation, and Yellow Hat, who attended seminars and lectures about leadership and shared their valuable opinions and experiences with me.

Students at Rikkyo University's Graduate School of Business Administration, who attended my "Leadership Theory" class, where we have learned about leadership together.

Mr. Akira Hayashi and Mr. Akira Imai, for reading the draft and giving me their valuable feedback.

Mr. Akira Miyahara, Mr. Ichihiko Ikegami, and Mr. Koichi Fuchino, who have given me advice at all times as mentors.

Ms. Fumiko Hayashi, the president of Tokyo Nissan; Mr. Tetsu Nakajima from Toyota; Mr. Jiro Nakazawa from Nippon Steel Corporation; and Mr. Yukihiko Seki from Panasonic, who constantly engage themselves in the management and personnel functions of their respective companies and have shared their deep knowledge and experiences with me.

Katsunori Takahashi, Mr. Katsuyuki Harui, Mr. Tatsutoshi Takanashi, Ms. Emiko Kashibo, and Ms. Chihiro Shinoda, who are associates of EQ Partners, which I started seven years ago, and who have helped me very much in writing this book.

Ms. Asako Fusano, a professional writer, who lent great support in the writing of this book.

Mr. Fumio Takano, for introducing me to the publisher.

Mr. Poh Shin, for his assistance in translating parts of the text in the book.

Most importantly, I would sincerely like to thank you, the reader, for reading this book.

I hope that this book will help you improve your leadership skills or give you some ideas for improving your professional and personal lives.

It would be great if everyone could become a World-Class Leader and lead himself or herself, team, society and globally, with value-creating dreams, thoughts, and beliefs.

I hope the world in and after the 21st century will become a great world for everyone to live in.

If you have any comments or opinions about this book, please contact me at my e-mail address. I look forward to hearing from you.

Tetsuya Abe
February, 2009
admin@eqpartners.com

INTRODUCING THE EQ PARTNERS

EQ Partners was established in 2002 with a heartfelt hope of cultivating better personnel and developing leadership through the cooperation of all people, including customers, as "EQual Partners." I feel that companies and society have a greater need for human cultivation and leadership development because of today's complex, diversified, globalized, and time-shortened business environment. We provide support to our customers for leadership development, MBA skill development, and global human resource development.

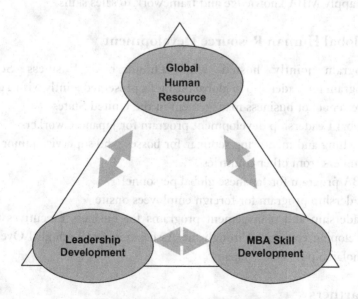

EQ Partners' three business domains

(1) Leadership Development

- Program for cultivating leaders and management executives for the next generation
- Leadership seminars for each level (from young staff members to executives)
- Coaching and mentoring seminars
- Business Emotional Quotient seminars
- Business communication seminars
- Remote Leadership seminars (leadership toward skills for junior staff members in remote locations)

(2) MBA Skill Development

- Practical 1-day MBA program
  To learn MBA subjects such as strategies, marketing, accounting in one day
- Practical MBA series for direct strengthening of sales and business skills
  To apply MBA knowledge and framework to sales skills

(3) Global Human Resource Development

- Program jointly hosted with Thunderbird Business School
  Program for leadership in global business, presented jointly with a graduate school of business management in the United States
- Global Leadership development program for Japanese workers
- Coaching and mentoring seminar for bosses who supervise junior staff members from other countries
- MBA program for Japanese global personnel
- Leadership program for foreign employees onsite
- Leadership and management programs for business executives from developing countries through the Association for Technical Overseas Scholarship (ATOS), Japan

EQ Partners

EQ Partners, Inc. www.eqpartners.com/eng
E-mail: admin@eqpartners.com

INTRODUCING THE CRAM SCHOOL KOKOROZASHI JYUKU

In a rapidly changing world, in which we cannot foresee the future, it is important for everyone to have some kind of inspiration to lead a quality life. In January 2009, I started a sort of adult cram school called Kokorozashi Jyuku, to provide a place where people with aspirations can learn together. I hope that this bringing together of individuals with aspirations will help to build a wave of change, a new era, as with the Meiji Restoration.

Qualifications for Participation

Individuals with aspirations (regardless of nationality, sex, age, or occupation)

Details

We hold a session in Shinagawa, Tokyo every month. We invite lecturers from elsewhere or take turns to deliver lectures ourselves. Topics covered include skills, know-how, experience, and thoughts that help us realize our dreams. The purpose of the school is to work and learn together through discussions with the lecturers and students. Participation is free of charge, except for shared expenses such as rental of the meeting venue.

Application

Please make enquiry to the person in charge of the Kokorozashi Jyuku at EQ Partners via e-mail.

Kokorozashi Jyuku

EQ Partners, Inc.
www.eqpartners.com
E-mail: admin@eqpartners.com

ABOUT THE AUTHORS

Tetsuya Abe

Chief Executive Officer of EQ Partners.

Lecturer (Leadership Theory) at Rikkyo University Graduate School, Tokyo, Japan.

Born in Fukuoka, graduated from Shuyukan High School and Chuo University School of Law, Tokyo, Japan.

Graduated with Master's Degree in Business Administration from the Graduate School of Bond University, Australia

Worked at Matsushita Electric Industry (Panasonic) in the fields of domestic sales, marketing, planning system engineering, overseas sales, and trading. Worked as the first resident officer in Hong Kong at the International Commercial Head Office of the company for trading business between Hong Kong, China, Japan and the West, for five years from 1996.

Established EQ Partners and assumed the office of Representative President of the company, held up to the present day.

Conducts human resource and organization consulting sessions and human resource development seminars for companies and universities with the business mission of "contributing to the creation of a better society through the development of leadership."

Started the cram school Kokorozashi Jyuku in January 2009 to cultivate people with high ideals.

Consulting and Seminars

(1) Human Resource Development Consulting
Consulting business regarding "the Individual and the Organization."
(2) Human Resource Development Seminar
Leadership Development; Cultivation and Training program for management executives and leaders for the next generation; World-Class Leadership Development; Coaching Seminar.
(3) Executive Coaching for executives and managers of companies. Provides support for management strategy planning, business problem, and problem solutions.

Clients and Employers

Toshiba Group companies, NEC Group companies, Fuji Film, NTT Group, Kao Customer Marketing, Sony, Sumitomo Corporation, Morinaga, Teijin, Yellow Hat, Casio, Cannon, Fujikura, Citibank, Tsumura, Japanese securities corporations, foreign-affiliated pharmaceutics companies, foreign-affiliated cosmetics companies, foreign-affiliated jewelry companies, foreign-affiliated financial companies, public offices, Japan Management Association, PHP Interface, The Research Institute of Marketing, Rikkyo University Graduate School, Nagoya Gakuin University…

Books

"*Carlos Ghosn's Way: Skills of Leadership Coaching*" (Asa Publishing Co. Ltd.)
"*Training Book for Learning Coaching Skills*" (Sogo Horei Publishing Co. Ltd.)

Contact

EQ Partners, Inc.
www.eqpartners.com
E-mail: admin@eqpartners.com

Sachin Chowdhery

- Director, Change Co., Ltd.
- Chairman, Abacus Venture Solutions Pvt Ltd.
- Managing Director of ITTR Co., Ltd.
- First overseas member and representative of
- The Associated Chambers of Commerce and Industry of India
- Member of The Tokyo Chamber of Commerce and Industry
- JTB Alliance Partner
- Visiting Professor at Kobe Institute of Computing (GSIT)

Biography

Sachin Chowdhery was born in New Delhi, India in 1973. Since his father was an Indian diplomat in Japan, he spent his childhood in that country. After he completed his graduation in India, he became an interpreter/coordinator at the Japan-based Destination Management company in India. He returned to Japan in 1996 to work at the same company in Tokyo. During this time, he achieved record high sales for two consecutive years. Soon after, he worked at a Japanese telecom and IT company, and again achieved a record high sales. In 2001, he founded Success TRC Co., Ltd. — an IT consulting service, system development and Destination Management company and became its Managing Director.

In 2002, the IT business of his company expanded as a result of the partnership with an Indian conglomerate Espire Group. In 2003, he conducted IT business seminars for companies like Dai Nippon Printing, NEC, Fujitsu etc in India. During this time, he also conducted seminars on sales strategies, marketing and confidence building for business entrepreneurs. He conducted seminars, lectures and training sessions on cross cultural global management for companies like Nissan, NEC, Fujitsu, Yokogawa Denki, Sumitomo Mitsui Banking Corporation Consulting, Kobe Steel, JTB, Toshiba, Hitachi.

He delivers lectures on Indian market and IT business in colleges and companies. He also provides consulting service to Japanese companies that are interested in starting a new business in India. In 2007, he founded Masterpiece Espire India Co., Ltd. This was the the first call center company for Japan in India. In January 2009, he founded Abacus Venture Solutions Pvt Ltd and ITTR Co., Ltd. In same year, he merged the IT team of Success TRC with Change Co., Ltd. He is currently the director of Change Co., Ltd.

Media/Writing

- "The Success of IT Business in Japan" (Tokyo Newspapers)
- "The IT Power and BRICS of India" (appeared in TBS)
- Opens seminars on "Marketing and Confidence — Make Them Your Sales Point"
- "Business Partnership with JTB and IT Seminars Started" (Nikkei Industrial Newspapers)
- "Seminars for IT Companies Started" (Soft Jinmyaku)
- "Project Management Seminars Started" (Business Computer News)
- "Business Therapy (Written by Hitoshi Aoki, Published by PHP)" (Introducing the story of Sachin Chowdhery in the section of IT industry in India.)
- Nikkei Newspaper on 23rd February. ITTR-related.
- Featured in *Gachiri Monday* in September 2004
- Featured in *Aera Biz.*
- Featured in *Cambria Kyuden* on June 6th 2010
- Featured in *Nikkei Money* in September 2010.

INTRODUCTION

The constant changes in today's fast-paced world demand world-class leadership. Leaders who integrate strategy (communication and direction with leadership), change (doing work in a different way), and transition (helping people adapt) will be more successful compared to those who do not. Learn what is required to develop world-class leaders throughout your constantly-changing organization.

World-class organizations believe in vision and common values that are shared by all members of the organization. In world-class companies that have a global focus, leaders are not "bosses", but rather "leaders" that people want to follow and who have the ability to create a world which people want to belong to. This style of leadership utilizes various leadership strategies to successfully translate visions into action.

What strategies must a leader employ to lead their organization to world-class recognition? What are the elements making up a world-class leader that allow for a more visionary approach? The essence of a world-class leader lies in his or her strategies for success in areas such as communications, personal relationships, cultural elements, and the management of change.

What are the leadership strategies needed for world-class leadership? To address this question, a research questionnaire was sent to over 250 businesses and organizations, seeking their insights into the leadership strategies needed for a leader to lead an organization that aspires to be recognized as world-class. World-class leaders follow the advice of Napoleon Hill, "You are searching for the magic key that will unlock the door to the source of power; and yet you have the key in your own hands. And you may make use of it the moment you learn to control your thoughts." World-class leadership is about learning to use these keys (strategies) effectively to develop world-class organizations.

Our research has led us to identify ten emerging leadership strategies. When used effectively, these strategies help recognize a world-class organization.

The strategies are listed below:

1. **Strategy for communication** — Good leadership is mostly good communication (Clutterback, 2002).
2. **Strategy to build integrity and trust** — A leadership strategy to build and maintain integrity must be a part of the foundation. Trust is described as the foundation for "the four cornerstones of moral leadership" (Clawson, 2002).
3. **Strategy for creating relationships** — In today's business world, the ability to create relationships is of paramount importance. Leaders should foster relationships with their customers, employees, staff, community, suppliers, peers and competitors.
4. **Strategy for change** — Change is about travelling from the old to the new, leaving yesterday for a new tomorrow (DeJager, 2001). The role of the world-class leader is to challenge the status quo, identify opportunities for improvement and implement change to achieve performance that improves constantly.
5. **Strategy for teamwork** — Teamwork can increase a leader's effectiveness, improve morale and productivity, and harness the skills of the organization's members.
6. **Strategy to grow leaders and produce champions** — Leaders who consistently pass on their strengths to others increase the overall intellectual capital of the organization.
7. **Strategy for building a world-class organizational culture** — Organizational culture serves as a common basis for understanding, interaction, and growth.
8. **Strategy for risk-taking** — The manager has his eyes set on the bottom line. The leader has his eyes set on the horizon (Parker, 2001).
9. **Strategy for quick action and quick decisions** — Leaders make quick decisions. Businesses require quick decisions where immediate action is critical. Therefore, more than inputs, quick action and immediate compliance become the need of the hour.

10. **Strategy for creating and implementing a shared vision** — Leaders create new ideas and implement these ideas with the people or business partners with whom they share their vision. With more ideas, a team of leaders with a shared vision can create dynamic leadership.

A review of the literature provided additional insights into these ten leadership strategies.

1. Strategy for Communication

"Leaders do not have a choice about whether or not to communicate. They only have a choice about how much to manage what they communicate" (Edgar Schein).

A world-class leader is someone whose actions have the most profound consequences on other people's lives because they have the ability to communicate. Communication is an invincible strategy necessary for world-class leadership. This sharing of profound knowledge, for better or worse, impacts lives forever. This ability to communicate effectively makes an enormous difference in employees' attitudes toward the organization as a whole.

Effective leaders/managers (1) set mutual expectations clearly (2) make sure everyone has very clear objectives and performance measures and check that they understand them (3) are good at planning and at communicating where the team is now and where it needs to be (4) give continuous feedback (5) set goals and ensure they have all the support they need from the manager and their colleagues (6) ensure that achievements are recognized, both within and outside the team (7) encourage and establish team members' sense of self-belief" (Schein).

For an organization to achieve world-class status, having a strategy for an effective communication program is important. Communication will play a key role, as it affects worker morale, productivity and performance, organizational change, and corporate identity. A quote from John Darling (1999) supports this statement, "Communication creates meaning for people in organizations, or at least it should. Getting the correct and intended message across at every level is an important key."

The benefits of communication are increased commitment to the organization's vision, greater cooperation throughout the organization by creating synergy and teamwork; improved employee morale; and employees feeling appreciated, recognized, and motivated to reach out to others in the organization. Communication is a defining element of an organization's culture. It is through that defining element that we find trust — our next strategy in the building of world-class leadership.

2. Strategy to Build Integrity and Trust

Trust is essential in everyday life and in any human relationship. Trust is about personal integrity and honor. World-class leadership may be defined as the level of trust that has been established and the positive products associated with that trust.

We find in Tyco, Enron, and Worldcom the results of the lack of trust. "World-class organizations and world-class leaders are moving from a culture of fear to a culture of trust" (Marshall, 2000).

3. Strategy for Creating Relationships

Relationships are very important in everyday life. Establishing relationships with employees, customers, suppliers, vendors, and even one's competitors enables an organization to be more responsive and proactive in meeting organizational goals and objectives. Fostering relationships is also just as important for world-class leaders as a means to achieve the organization's mission. Leaders need to focus the energy and resources of the organization towards attaining world-class results.

Strong and effective relationships are based on trust and respect that both parties have for one another. "Trust affects power. It changes the balance of power in relationships. Trust between people increases security and potential while it lasts. Trust produces vulnerability to risk of betrayal and failure" (Ward, 2003).

Managing relationships is critical to understanding the needs, desires, and expectations of the people around you.

4. Strategy for Change

World-class leadership demonstrates the most effective strategies for change. The knowledge of the way the world marketplace is changing in relation to where we are and where we wish to go makes it imperative for the world-class leader to adapt a strategy for change. We all recognize that we live in a time of accelerating change, and the only way to survive is to adapt to change. The need for understanding change, therefore, is critical because organizations worldwide are confronting more turbulent markets, more demanding stakeholders, more discerning customers, and a very different marketplace compared to the situation just two years ago. The role of a world-class leader is to challenge the status quo, identify opportunities for improvement, and implement change in a bid to achieve better performance in every aspect of business.

5. Strategy for Teamwork

With the challenge and complexity of business today, it is difficult for any leader to lead alone; he or she needs help from others. Teamwork helps increase a leader's effectiveness, improve morale and productivity, and harness the skills of the organization's members. Geoff Unwin, Chairman of Cap Gemini SA, said that he relies heavily on teamwork and works with other people to accomplish his goals. Not only do teams enable him to reach his desired goals, they also produce higher quality results (Ashby and Miles, 2002).

Teamwork enables generation of ideas and thoughts on how to solve a problem or increase productivity. Leaders who encourage teamwork are able to fully utilize the additional skills and ideas of others. Leveraging the skills and ideas of several employees, instead of just one, increases the speed and accuracy with which problems can be solved and leads to increased productivity. Sims *et al.* (1999) documented the implementation and activities of teams at the customer service center for the IDS financial services organization. Without supervisor assistance, team members developed and implemented process improvements that reduced the time needed to answer the phone during peak periods from 7.5 minutes to 13 seconds.

Kotter (1999) observed, "Because managerial work is increasingly a leadership task, and because leaders operate through a complex web of dependent relationships, managerial worth is increasingly becoming a game of informal dependence on others instead of just formal power over others." World-class leaders in today's business world operate in a very fast-paced environment filled with numerous opportunities and challenges on several fronts. Leaders must address these opportunities and challenges if their organization is to survive and prosper. Even if they possess many of the skills needed to be effective in their leadership role, it is often difficult, if not impossible, for the leader to address the issues. Leaders must actively encourage teamwork at all levels to in the organization. Having a strategy for teamwork will enable leaders at all levels to integrate teamwork into their inventory of effective strategies for the growth and success of the organization.

6. Strategy to Grow Leaders to Produce Champions

We constantly hear that people are the most important asset an organization has, and that their effectiveness is the key to success. Growing leaders is an integral strategy for world-class organizations and, consequently, world-class leaders. The development of leaders within an organization can have a dramatic effect on the organization's culture, growth, productivity, market share, and even profit. According to Jim Krug, a consultant with the Development Institute of Denver, Colorado, "…approximately 75 percent of leadership development occurs on the job" (Krug, 1996). This shows us that in many instances, leadership is being taught in an organizational setting, rather than in an academic setting. A world-class organization must have the right strategy to grow leaders and produce champions.

Leadership development needs to be related to the organization's strategies and goals (Zenger, 2000). One of the comments in the literature that is often repeated is that leadership needs to focus on connecting to the company's values and goals. In the leadership development process, the organization needs to fully identify and then communicate the strategies to the managers or associates who are to be trained. Additionally, leadership needs to be connected with the organizational culture. Another area of focus for growing leaders is to provide realistic training scenarios for individuals attending leadership training programs. The literature points to the importance of training programs that use theory to train leaders, instead of practice. As Edward Deming points out, it is through the development of a theory that we learn new and profound knowledge.

Several large world-class corporations are taking senior leadership involvement to the next level by having senior officers conduct the training themselves. The CEO of PepsiCo, Roger Enrico, spends 100 days a year running Pepsi's leadership development program for top management. "The central idea is simple: the most important responsibility of a leader is to personally develop other leaders" (Tichy and DeRose, 1996).

Growing a leader is not something an organization should embark upon hastily for short-term success. It takes time, commitment, determination and a strategy. It requires a solid foundation with proper planning, use of the organizational culture, proper training methods and individuals with the right stuff, potential, and desire to excel in world-class leadership.

7. Strategy for Building a World-Class Organizational Culture

What is organizational culture? It is not a list of values developed by senior management and placed in a frame on the office wall or elsewhere in the office. Organizational culture is, in essence, a set of basic rules or guidelines to give members of the group or organization a common basis for understanding and interacting with each other (Goleman, 2002). Culture is a phenomenon that surrounds us all. It helps us understand and define an organization by focusing on its values, behavior, norms, and traditions. The values, norms and integrity of a workforce define the organization as it is perceived from within and by the outside world. Organizational culture appears to be the operating system of an organization and guides how employees think, act and feel. World-class leaders should be conscious of this culture and guide it in a positive manner.

John Kotter's work places further emphasis upon the centrality of corporate culture. In describing, "what leaders really do," he cites these concerns as a central theme for a leader who is engaged in a program of change. In his "Ten Observations About Managerial Behavior," Kotter notes that failures to effect meaningful change arise when leaders fail in "anchoring changes in the corporation's culture" or when they fail "to sufficiently connect new approaches to the culture or to create new cultures that can support these approaches" (Kotter, 1999).

Today the pace of change is very rapid, particularly in high tech industries. Only organizations that can adapt to this fast-changing environment can survive. The secret to an organization being able to manage both change and continuity lies in the leaders' understanding and their ability to influence the organization's culture to fit its strategic goals.

Effective leadership, with regard to cultural interactions and development, is crucial in fostering an atmosphere of success. Spragins (2003) sums it up quite well, "To that end, we looked for managers who find novel ways to demonstrate how deeply they value their employees." The strategy for world-class leadership that is utilized in the dissemination, understanding, and development of an organization's culture is a vital part of the skill set required to make a great leader. "Understanding how the culture of an organization impacts the bottom line and profitability of a company can be revealing. Companies can maximize their profitability by defining all the elements of their culture, deciding if they like what they discover, assessing whether their behavior and actions are supportive of the culture, and conducting thorough assessments of personnel to ensure they fully embrace the culture of their organization" (Bliss, 2003, p. 9).

Clearly, one of the principal tasks of the world-class leader is to ensure that his/her group fosters an appropriate and positive culture. Obviously, there is no single "right" culture, so this aspect of leadership is fraught with difficulty. However, in order to aspire to world-class leadership, any potential leader should place heavy emphasis upon creating or nurturing a positive organizational culture and on eliminating negative culture influences.

8. Strategy for Risk-Taking

In the 18th century, Samuel Johnson said that taking risks is worthwhile because it is the "risk of the certainty of little for the chance of much." These days, risk is seen as a negative thing, and people put in a lot of effort to minimize their risks in all things they do. For leaders who presumably have their eyes set on a successful future, risk becomes something less philosophical. As Samuel Johnson says "risk is an endeavor that is very much worth understanding and embracing as a part of their leadership mentality from the beginning".

Is risk-taking a key strategy for world-class leadership? I believe that research would strongly indicate that the capacity for taking risks of many kinds is a necessary function of sound leadership and managerial practice. Companies and their leaders need to be comfortable taking risks simply in order to survive in the marketplace. Responding to the economic factors that affect a business, and being able to reasonably anticipate the needs and demands of the future, requires a significant amount of risk. Innovation and development of new products and the confidence to pursue and market them is based heavily on risks of failure. Survival, success, and happiness would appear to be intrinsically connected to the ability to manage, lead, and undertake risk.

Attitudes toward risk also have a big influence on decision making. Risk-averters are inclined towards "safe" strategies in which external threats appear minimal, profits are adequate though not spectacular, and there are adequate in-house resources to meet anticipated needs. They may view pioneering-type innovations as too chancy compared to proven, well-established techniques. Risk-averters place a high value on strategies that minimize downside risks.

Eager risk-takers lean more towards opportunistic strategies where the payoffs are greater, the challenges are more demanding, and the glamor is more appealing, despite chances of failure. A risk-taker prefers innovation to imitation, and a focus on a strategic offensive ranks ahead of defensive conservatism. A confident optimism about market prospects overrules pessimism, and attempts to improve the firm's market position are more attractive than maintaining status quo.

Since world-class leaders presumably have their eyes set on being successful in the future, they need to focus on understanding risk and developing a strategy for risk-taking.

9. Strategy for Quick Action and Quick Decisions

Leaders make quick decisions. They do not wait or think; they just do things. They make use of right opportunities at the right time.

It is important to have a product plan, a good business strategy, and analyses of competitors. Do not expect to be perfect. Leave room for a margin of error and do not be afraid to pivot quickly if your leadership requires you to do so. You can not be a world-class leader without taking any risks — if you were really that safe you would not be making a quick decision: you could be staying in the comfort zone.

10. Strategy for Creating and Implementing a Vision

The world-class leader is a visionary. Visionary leaders use their unique leadership insights to develop a vision and convince others in the organization to support and help reach new heights or world-class status. The development of a visionary strategy will determine where the gaps are, where the organization is, and the levels it can reach. Vision places emphasis on what is and what can be. Vision is a must-have for every world-class leader.

In their article, "*Multi-level visioning*" Yearout, Miles, and Koonce (2001) note that, "Once there is clarity and agreement among leaders on where they want to take the organization, the challenge is to enlist the help of employees." They suggest five steps for world-class leaders to realize their vision. First, establish positive tension in the organization by showing the members the vision of where you want to take the company and where it stands as of now. This positive tension will motivate employees to realize the vision and help the organization attain a world-class status. Second, leverage lessons from the past. Knowing what worked well in the past can help the organization reach out to the stakeholders in a positive way, while still recognizing the need for change.

Sachin Chowdhery

➤ CHAPTER 1 ◄

OVERVIEW OF LEADERSHIP

1. Three Waves of Change: Changes in the Business Environment from the 20th Century to the 21st Century

1.1. *Internetization*

Since the incorporation of Internet function in Microsoft's Windows™ software for personal computers in 1995, the use of the Internet has spread rapidly. According to 2007 data, about 70 million people in Japan (i.e. more than 60% of the entire population) and about 700 million people worldwide (i.e. more than 10% of the entire population) use the Internet for business and in daily life. It can be said that business people who do not use the Internet are exceptions.

The Internet will continue to spread ever wider, and the era is almost here where almost everyone in business and social activities would use this medium. What will happen if the Internet becomes widely used by every level of the society?

The Internet had, and continues to have an immense impact on the society — companies, organizations, and our daily life. For example, there are almost no digital divides (i.e. the gap between people who have effective access to digital and information technology and those with very limited or no access at all). Any individual, whether a top executive, manager, mid-career or junior or even part-time employee, whether inside or outside of the country can obtain the same (or at least very similar) information and knowledge previously available to only a selective few, such as top executives or leaders.

If society can change to such an extent, so can the type of leadership. In the past, top executives and leaders held most of the information and knowledge which was then used to make unilateral leadership decisions to lead their members.

But in the Internet era, an increasing number of members or followers have access to the same information and knowledge as their leaders. For this reason, it is more effective for all the leaders and followers to take on main roles of leadership.

1.2. *Globalization*

According to the 2000 BRICS report by the American investment company Goldman Sachs, the BRIC countries — Brazil, Russia, India and China — are seen to be undergoing rapid economic growth and taking on major roles in the world economy due to their large population and rich resources and markets. The 2050 prediction economic scale has ranked China as no. 1, followed by U.S.A., and India respectively.

In fact, not only BRIC countries but also NEXT11 — which includes Indonesia and Vietnam and other countries in Asia, East Europe, South America, the Middle East, and Africa — are achieving rapid economic growth. These countries are trying to catch up with the developed countries that have long dominated world economies, such as the U.S.A., Japan, and European countries.

Japan experienced rapid economic growth after WWII, helping it to catch up with or even overtake some western countries. Similarly, at present, developing countries are catching up with the advanced countries and progressing at a greater pace than their predecessors did.

A top management executive of an electronics manufacturer, who is in charge of its business in China, has commented that China merely took one or two years to catch up and reach levels that took Japan and other developed countries approximately five to over ten years to achieve. For example, Japan spent decades developing television technology from monochrome CRT TVs to color CRT TVs and then to flat-screen LCD TVs. In comparison, by studying the leading-edge technologies from Japan and other developed countries, China can start from the level of the latest flat-screen LCD televisions. Similarly, other latecomers can catch up with their predecessors at a rapid pace.

Moreover, many companies are trying to expand their business beyond national borders — General Electric, IBM, Procter & Gamble, Starbucks Coffee, Google, and Amazon, to name a few.

Consider, for example, a leader who does business in Tokyo. To provide suitable leadership to his/her followers, he/she cannot restrict the competitors and market within the population of 10 million in Tokyo or 120 million in Japan. He/she would need to consider the population of 600 million in the developed countries in the West, if not the 6.3 billion in the entire world. These population figures are 600 times higher than that of Tokyo and 55 times higher than that of Japan. Customers and competitors are no longer confined within a certain area or country but are now spread across national borders. A leadership approach executed for a limited area or individual country can no longer be employed.

On the other hand, in terms of market coverage, a business can now be expanded worldwide instead of being limited to only one area or just to Japan. From that perspective, globalization promises a big chance along with a big challenge.

Thus, unlike in the 20th century, exercising leadership now requires any company, any organization, and any individual to heighten the awareness and understanding of the whole world.

1.3. *Diversification*

Earlier, Japanese companies and society strived to maintain strict homogeneity. The approach was Japanese-centric, male-centric, and senior-centric, and organizations consisted of people who had similar experience and views. This was certainly a strong point of societies and organizations in Japan.

But for nearly 20 years, since the early 1990s, there has been an economic downturn. This climate has seen corporate downsizings, as well as the diversification of employment, employing strategies such as recruiting female employees, temporary staff, part-time workers, and foreign workers. In addition, the reach of human resources has gone global.

The leadership style of the 20th century tended to be along the lines of "Just watch my back and follow me!" and "Hang in there, for now! Good things [promotions, raises] are on your way," with an attitude of "They won't quit their jobs, even if they have to put up with some things they don't like."

But because of the changes in the business environment, these approaches will no longer work. Leaders who pursue 20th-century-type

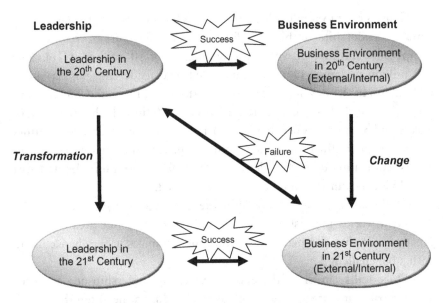

Figure 1.1.   Changes in business environment and leadership

20th Century	21st Century
• Local market centered	• Global market
• Pyramid-type organization	• Network-type organization
• Slow changes	• Complicated/accelerated changes
• Simple business environment	• Complicated business environment
• Gathering of relatively similar human resources	• Diversity of human resources

Figure 1.2.   20th century versus 21st century

leadership styles have been experiencing a hard time in leading their followers; the followers' motivation is in a slump, or in some cases, they have quit their jobs.

In fact, in Japan today nearly 35% — more than one out of three — of the newly recruited college graduate employees quit their jobs within three years.

2. Four Levels of Leadership

Now the begging question is, "What kind of leadership is required to over-come and survive these three waves — and to bring it one step ahead by putting these three waves into motion at its fullest potential."

In this book, leadership is divided into four levels:

(1) Self-Leadership
(2) Team Leadership
(3) Global Leadership
(4) Social Leadership

2.1. *Self Leadership*

These four levels of leadership define world-class leadership. Self-Leadership means "understanding and leading yourself." The importance and posture of Self-Leadership changing in the 21st century.

Due to the advent of the internet, anyone can obtain any amount of information. A blend of two of the waves — internetization and globalization — is changing business work days to 24 hours a day, seven days a week.

Time zone differences allow business and social activities to go on ceaselessly, 24/7, from Japan to Asia to India to the Middle East to Europe/Africa to the Americas, and back to Japan again. In such situations, you could lose yourself, become overwhelmed, or throw your work life off-balance if you do not understand and lead yourself — that is, putting yourself on the right track.

To exercise a stable leadership in such an ever-changing environment and to lead yourself, you will need Self-Leadership — the ability to lead yourself to achieve your goals, create new value in society, and improve your life. It is very important to be able to exercise Self-Leadership in the 21st century and beyond.

In the 20th century, societies, companies, and organizations, to some extent, set the direction of an individual's progress in terms of life and work. For example, a person entering a company at trainee level might generally be able to expect a proper job in three years, become a supervisor in five years, a manager in ten years, and then a general manager.

In the 21st century, by contrast, there are fewer instances in which such a structure is in place. And even if it exists, individuals still need to have a deep understanding of their own strengths and weaknesses and their own sense of values, as well as understanding the societies, companies, and organizations, to lead both as individuals and groups.

This Self-Leadership becomes the foundation of the entire leadership array.

(This will be discussed in depth in Chapter 2.)

2.2. Team Leadership (understand/lead a team)

In the 21st century, the nature of organizations and teams has been changing as well. Team Leadership concerns understanding and leading an organization or a team.

Team Leadership requires the following three actions:

- Analyze the environment you are in, and establish the team's direction (Vision).
- Get the team to take action towards the direction (Action).
- Get the team to learn and grow more through experience (Learning).

For most of the 20th century, one company's vision was almost the same as that of another company. The action was a one-way order from a supervisor downward to a subordinate, and the learning was also one-way teaching from a supervisor downward to a subordinate.

However, in the 21st century, the vision needs to be unique, interesting, and different from that of other companies. To accomplish the vision, action should be taken in line with the plans conceived by all the team members. Moreover, learning must take place in a variety of directions, such as between supervisors and subordinates, among co-workers, and between people within and outside of the company.

In addition, because of the effects of the three waves of change, the style of Team Leadership that was popular in the past, in which a leader gives an order and team members follow it, is no longer applicable. Thus, a new type of Team Leadership is needed.

Now, it is vital to put team strength ahead of individual strength and to learn as a team rather than just as individuals.

(This will be discussed in depth in Chapter 3.)

2.3. *Global Leadership (understand/lead globally)*

Because of the three waves of change, the Global Leadership of the world becomes more important in the future. This is a new type of leadership in which action is taken by examining, considering, and understanding the economics, customers, competitors, and related parties on a global scale.

In the past, a company's competitors were within the same area or the same country, whereas today the competitors could be anywhere in the world. For example, in the past, a coffee shop competed only with other individual coffee shops in the same area. But now it must compete with nationwide coffee shop chains such as Doutor in Japan and worldwide chains such as Starbucks and Tully's.

For electronic products, such as televisions and audio devices, Panasonic had Japanese companies, such as Sony, Hitachi, and Toshiba, as its competitors. Now their competition has spread worldwide to include Samsung and LG Electronics from Korea and Haier from China.

Earlier, only management executives and people dealing with the overseas business needed to think globally, but today everyone needs to think globally to survive. On the other hand, if we can manage to put globalization to our use, we stand a big chance of attaining global success, to an extent never dreamed of before.

(This will be discussed in depth in Chapter 4.)

2.4. *Social Leadership (understand/lead society)*

Recently, social problems such as food product mislabeling, financial crises, global warming, and energy issues are occurring both in Japan and worldwide.

The important element linking these social problems is the problem of leadership. The quality of leadership has a great impact on the occurrence and solution of these kinds of problems.

Akira Miyahara, former representative director of Fuji Xerox, said, "One should aspire to be a good member of society before becoming a good business leader or business person."

To be a good member of society, every individual should take action after such examination and take into consideration the entire society. Similarly, a leader should promote such social-mindedness to all team members.

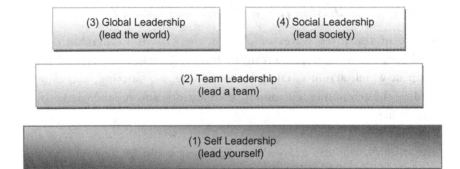

Figure 1.3.   Overview of World-Class Leadership

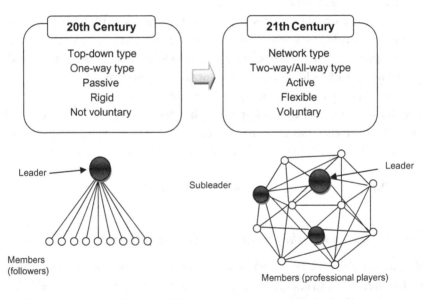

Figure 1.4.   Leadership in the 20th century versus leadership in the 21st century

Though we discuss Social Leadership in the last chapter of the book, this leadership is the main premise underlying the other leadership modes. (This will be discussed in depth in Chapter 5.)

➤ CHAPTER 2 ◄

SELF-LEADERSHIP

1. What is Self-Leadership? (WHAT)

In this book, "leadership" is defined as "guiding yourself, your team, the world, and society in a better direction."

There are four levels of leadership:

(1)   Self-Leadership (to lead yourself)
(2)   Team Leadership (to lead a team)
(3)   Global Leadership (to lead globally)
(4)   Social Leadership (to lead the society)

In this chapter, we will first discuss Self-Leadership, the ability to lead yourself.

Self-Leadership is "the ability to lead yourself in a better direction in order to achieve objectives or create value." This entails defining what you want to achieve, such as your dreams and visions for the future, and the values that you want to uphold, as well as finding and understanding your current strengths and weaknesses and likes and dislikes.

2. Why is Self-Leadership Needed? (WHY)

The nature of Self-Leadership has changed greatly since the last decade of the 20th century. In the past, usually the society, company, organization, and/or superiors at work guided people to some extent in the direction they would go. In the past, most companies in Japan provided lifetime employment and promotions were based on seniority. Therefore, one generally progressed in a company from a newly-hired to a mid-career employee, and then from an administrative position to a management position. By climbing this ladder, an employee was expected to grow as a working member of the society. Moreover, the business environment of the 20th century was not as complicated as it is at present, and change was not rapid. Accordingly, there was little need to review or alter direction.

However, in the 21st century, changes are occurring with dramatic speed. The very nature of modern society and its organizations has become so complex that comparisons cannot be made. The business environment of today is becoming internetized, globalized, diversified — and complicated. If you try to lead yourself without a good grasp of the situation or the position you are in, it might be difficult to succeed. Alternatively, if you can assess such an environment and lead yourself adroitly, you will be able to exercise Self-Leadership effectively by aligning the three waves of change, that is, internetization, globalization, and diversification, on your side.

The term "leadership" is generally understood as an activity exercised over other people, such as leading a team or its members. However, before exercising team leadership, you should be able to lead yourself well. If you do not understand and lead yourself well, you may make bad decisions as a leader. You may lose confidence in your actions and decisions and vacillate in what you say to your team members. Moreover, the direction of the leadership for the members or team may waver. As a result, your team members may be confused and may say:

"Our leader does not seem to be confident in what he/she is doing."
"Our leader is inconsistent because he/she changes what he/she says according to time and circumstances."
"What he/she says is of course right, but he/she is not acting accordingly."
"We do not feel like following this leader."

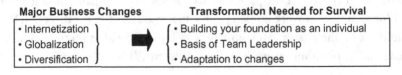

Figure 2.1. 21st century transformers

"We cannot trust the leader as a person."

"We do not want to be like the leader."

In such cases, your team members may be unwilling to follow or listen to you, and there will be no way you can bring your team to achieve the goal. In some companies, there have been instances where members would follow one leader but not another, even when both leaders give exactly the same directions. Conversely, if you have a good understanding of yourself and exercise Self-Leadership, you will be able to take the initiative in improving the business as well as exercising stable leadership over the team. The team members will feel that the leader is "reliable," "never vacillating," "trustworthy," and "a good person to work with."

Therefore, before leading a team, a leader should be able to exercise Self-Leadership effectively. To be specific, to "lead oneself" entails understanding what kind of missions or objectives, future visions, and/or values the leader has, whether he/she actually puts them into practice or takes action, and whether he/she continues to learn and grow. The latter involves learning by reading books on certain topics, learning from teachings by others, and learning through practice.

All successful leaders that I know of exercise Self-Leadership effectively. Without Self-Leadership, a leader cannot exercise Team Leadership. A person who cannot understand and lead oneself properly cannot understand or lead others. According to the Chinese philosopher Confucius,

"Knowing others is wisdom. Knowing yourself is cleverness,"

which means that although it is important to know others, it is even more important to know yourself.

3. How Do We Put Self-Leadership into Practice? (HOW)

How do we put into practice this "Self-Leadership" that becomes the foundation of all our leadership values?

The important elements for exercising each of the four levels of leadership (Self, Team, Global, and Social) are found in the three-part cycle of Direction, Action, and Learning. In other words, you will first determine the direction you need to go, take action towards that goal, and then learn from the actions. Then, you will determine a better direction, take action, and learn again, and the cycle goes on.

3.1. *Direction (Understand yourself)*

First, you need to gain a deep understanding of yourself from all perspectives. To do so, you will need to reflect on the incidents that happened in your past and what you thought and how you reacted during those incidents. Then, by asking questions such as

"What are my strengths?"
"What are my weaknesses or points to be improved?"
"What do I like and dislike?"
"What values are important to me?"
"What is my mission?"

and so on, you will learn about just what makes you yourself.

3.1.1. *Learn from your past*

In order to understand a country or the world, it is important to learn about its history. Similarly, to learn better about yourself, it is helpful to look back on your experiences. Specifically, list three experiences in your business or personal life that gave you the highest level of satisfaction and fulfillment. Then analyze why those experiences gave you a sense of accomplishment.

Drawing a self-history line is a method that helps you determine the values that are important. In this method, a line is plotted on a graph to show the level of fulfillment and satisfaction along a timeline (age) from birth, through school days, and until now. For example, perhaps the fulfillment level was high when you were working hard in your high school club activities but went down when you entered college, where you had a hard time making friends. Then, when you started working, the level of fulfillment went up as you did your best in your job but dipped when you were feeling downbeat because you did not get along well with your co-workers. Similarly, you can observe that the fulfillment level changes in accordance with time and age.

Experience or episode that brought you a high level of satisfaction and fulfillment (Example: Success of the A project.)	Reason (Example: Though it was my first experience and the hurdle was high, we accomplished it after overcoming difficulties.)
•	•
•	•
•	•

Figure 2.2. Self-history: Experience and satisfaction

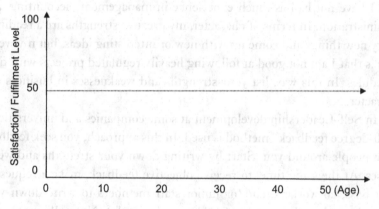

Figure 2.3. Self-history: Satisfaction and time

As you plot your line on the graph, write down details of the main episode of the time. This helps in analyzing whether your fulfillment level was high or low at that time. Your set of values will become clearer to you. For example, you may determine whether your fulfillment level is higher when you are working alone or as part of a team. Drawing a self-history line will help you discover the reasons for your highs and lows in the fulfillment level. This, in turn, will help you define what makes you feel fulfilled or satisfied. In this self-history line, rather than looking at absolute values for the high and low fulfillment levels, look for tendencies in the ups and downs. It is important to note the points that are especially high or low. When you draw the line, do it intuitively and freely, without thinking in depth. Then, write down the points you have noticed in plotting the line, such as turning points (situations when you changed) and the set of values you developed along the way.

• **Learn about your strengths and weaknesses, likes and dislikes**

Everyone has strengths and weaknesses, in business as well as in their basic character. By analyzing the strengths and weaknesses in depth, you will be able to learn about yourself. For example, my strengths in business are the experience and skills I have developed in sales and marketing at a major electronics company and in international trade. Conversely, my weakness is that I have not had as much experience in management, accounting, and administration. In terms of character, my greatest strengths are a readiness to try new things and come up with new or interesting ideas, but my weakness is that I am not good at following heavily regulated projects with tight schedules. In this way, list your strengths and weaknesses in business and character.

In Self-Leadership development at some companies and universities, a "360-degree feedback" method is used. In this approach, you seek feedback from people around you. Start by writing down your strengths and weaknesses. At the same time, to receive objective feedback, make a request to your boss, co-workers, and/or junior staff members to write down your strengths and weaknesses (preferably anonymously). Normally many people find such objective feedback from others very helpful. Some people would feel, "I had a feeling that I might be like that, but now I see that other people also see me that way too," or "Other people do perceive me in a very good light," or "Other people see strengths and weaknesses in me that I was not aware of myself." In any case, this is a very good tool for learning about and understanding yourself objectively.

In addition to strengths and weaknesses, feelings of like and dislike should also be considered. Some people may advise you never to have likes and dislikes in business, but the fact is, people that I know in business do have their likes and dislikes. People work energetically and have fun viscerally when they like what they do, and this makes it easier to produce good results. Conversely, many people who persevere in working at things they do not like become depressed, and this makes it difficult for them to produce good results. Therefore, to be more effective in exercising

Self-Leadership and achieving your goals, it is very important to know your likes and dislikes. For example, I love to do new things or things that other people have not done and to try out things that I come up with freely. Conversely, I am not very fond of doing things that anyone can do, things that are nothing special, or things that I must do according to the directions or orders of others. I like working energetically in a team with a variety of people, but I do not like working on things quietly by myself.

When you have to work on something you do not like, instead of just doing it grudgingly, it is important to find some meaning or enjoyment you can derive from it. This will have a positive effect on your achievement and growth.

"What values are most important to you?"
"What are the things that you will never compromise in leading yourself?"

3.2. *Direction (Lead yourself)*

Now that you have learned more about your strengths, weaknesses, likes, dislikes, and set of values by analyzing your past and present, let us think about your future dreams, visions, and missions.

One of the tools that can be used is "My Leadership Vision."

The WANT part at the top of the chart represents the things you have the will to do, and this relates to the "things you like." You may want to start with thinking about what you want to actualize and do. The CAN area at the bottom left represents things that you can do or that you may be able to do in the future. This relates to your strengths. Think deeply about the area where WANT and CAN overlap. But when you want to formulate visions and create goals, having just "things you can do" (strengths) and "things you want to do" (likes) is not enough. Another element is required, the NEED area at the bottom right, which represents what your team, company, or society wants from you.

So there are things you want to do and actualize (WANT), things you can do (CAN), and things that are required of you (NEED). The area where all these three parts overlap shows what you can do and want to do and what others expect you to do. This is the area in which you can work most effectively. As you determine your visions, it is good to think about the

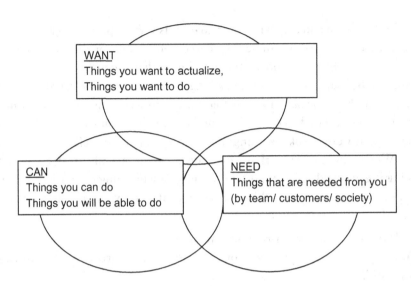

Figure 2.4. My leadership vision

three elements of what you can do, what you want to do, and what you are expected to do.

For example, when I left the company and started my own business, I wanted to work on leadership development in Japan, Asia, and the world. At that time, although I had experience in leading members in the sales and marketing divisions in the company, I did not have enough knowledge or the know-how to teach others about leadership systematically. Therefore, I explored the possibility of being able to teach systems of leadership to others in the future by assiduously studying leadership (CAN).

Also, ever since I was a kid, I have enjoyed (WANT) reading biographies about great people, such as Hideyo Noguchi, Ryoma Sakamoto, Gandhi, and Schweitzer, and learning about Japanese leaders, such as Konosuke Matsushita, the founder of Panasonic, and Soichiro Honda, the founder of Honda.

The quality of leadership shown by a leader has a tremendous effect on whether the country, company, or team is successful, that is, whether it grows or stagnates. Due to the globalization of the world economy and popularization of Internet technology throughout the world, we are in a rapidly changing era, and society as well as teams are more complicated. Because many leaders are required to lead teams in the right direction, I knew that the need for leadership development would increase in the future. And I have realized that human resource development and leadership development are assuming more significance. In the West, where countries lead in human resource development when compared to Japan, the need for these skills is increasing year after year (NEED).

Similarly, I believe that leadership development in Japan, Asia, and the world conforms to what I can do (CAN), what I want to do (WANT), and what I am expected to do (NEED). Therefore, I have been, and will be, focusing on and working on it with my utmost effort as my personal vision.

"What are the things you want to do (WANT), things you can do (CAN), and things you are expected to do (NEED)?"
"What is your future vision for yourself?"

4. The Elements of Self-Leadership

4.1. *Action (TO DO) model for Self-Leadership*

4.1.1. *GROW model*

How do we exercise Self-Leadership in actual practice? Let us look at the "GROW model" approach toward developing leadership.

"GROW" is an acronym in which each letter is the initial letter of an element required for leadership development.

G = Goal, including visions that you want to materialize.
R = Reality, from which you learn about your current strengths and weaknesses, likes and dislikes.
O = Option, the action plans for closing the gaps between the goal and the current situation; and
W = Will to move into action.

In Step 1 (Goal), think about your goals, or visions that you want to materialize, and what you want to be in three, five, or maybe ten years. Then, in Step 2 (Reality), analyze your current situation. You will surely find gaps (discrepancies) between your current strengths and those needed to achieve your goals. Step 3 (Option), action planning, deals with how to compensate for those discrepancies.

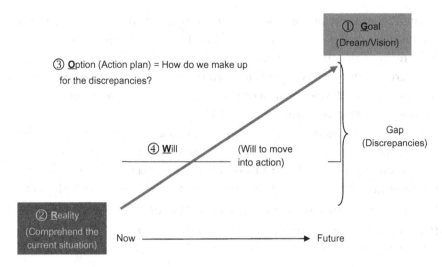

Figure 2.5. Self-Leadership development: The GROW model

Make an action plan by examining the current situation and comparing it to your objectives. For example, your objective may be to achieve great results overseas. But perhaps you feel that your current language skills are not good enough. To improve your language skills, you will need to determine the level to which you want to improve. Also, personal connections are vital in business overseas, and you may need to make an action plan to develop contacts with more people. Finally, in Step 4 (Will), you should commit to your will to move into action. When people actually take action, feelings and thoughts are very important. Once you assess your goal and current situation and formulate your action plan, it is crucial to ensure that you have committed your feelings and thoughts toward actualizing it.

It is a good idea to put this GROW model into regular practice. Check your goal, current situation, action plan, and will as often as possible. Many of the masters of Self-Leadership exercise this GROW model naturally by setting a goal for themselves and then constantly calling it to mind.

4.1.2. *Self-Leadership development model*

A method for moving forward with your Self-Leadership development is explained here.

First, it is necessary "to understand the fundamentals of leadership." If you do not know the basics of swimming or *kendo* (the art of Japanese fencing), you will not be able to improve quickly in that activity or your improvement may be limited even if you try hard. Similarly, it is important to understand the fundamental principles of leadership. When I started working in Hong Kong, I had the opportunity to exercise the right kind of leadership with the team members. Although I had previous experience in Japan, I had not yet acquired some of the basic knowledge, such as what I should and should not do. As a result, I was exercising "leadership in my own way," and hence was not able to work well with the local team members, and failed repeatedly. If I had known more about the basics of leadership at that time, I would have been able to provide better leadership to build a better team and promote our business better.

Second, it is important to know about yourself. Thinking things through on your own and then receiving feedback from others will help improve your Self-Leadership. Earlier, I cited the words of Confucius. Socrates also said "Know thyself" — that is, self-knowledge is crucial.

Third, to improve your leadership, it is important to learn from others. We learn from others as we grow in our relationships with them. You can learn from your boss, seniors, co-workers, and junior staff members at your company and get feedback from them. Having a mentor with whom you can discuss your dreams and troubles will help when you are having problems with your way of business operations or directions. For example, it may help to talk things over with your former boss or seniors at the company, seniors or classmates at school, or elders, who are chock-full of experiences and insights.

Prof. James Collins is a professor at Stanford University and the author of "Visionary Company," a best seller in the area of business management and leadership. He says that one of the most important ways to develop your leadership skills is to learn from your mentors. Prof. Collins reveals that by talking to his mentor, Mr. Peter Drucker, who is widely considered a great business scholar, he can enrich his knowledge by discovering and realizing new things even through the questions his mentor asks, not necessarily just by the answers he gives.

Furthermore, Mr. Jack Welch, an ex-CEO of General Electric, used to have several mentors as well and discussed specific technical matters with mentors who specialised in those fields. Also, a research study has shown that more than 80% of business managers at Japanese companies have some sort of a mentor they can consult. Many business managers, such as Jack Welch, in addition to stimulating independent thinking, also improve themselves by consulting their mentors. I recommend the same to you.

Similar to the mentor resource, it is also good to get help from a coach. What is the difference between a mentor and a coach? A mentor is someone you can consult and talk things over with and who has a great deal of experience, skills, or know-how in a certain area. Similarly, a coach, usually someone at a senior level, has more experience in life and business and can tell you about their experience or give you advice. In addition, regardless of his/her experience, skills, or know-how, a coach will take on the role of actively helping you in bringing out your potential and organizing it. By talking to a coach or having a coach ask you various questions, you can think and learn about yourself and grow. Thus, learning from others is also crucial.

I put my effort into improving my own leadership skills all the time by consulting with several mentors and coaches.

Learn the basics, know about yourself, and learn from others. The most important part is to make an action plan and put it into practice. Even if you have a brilliant thought or idea, you will not achieve anything if you do not take action. People who have great ideas but they do not take action will never improve themselves as leaders, and others will lose their faith in them.

All the leaders I have observed so far take action boldly without harboring doubts. When they cannot see a clear view ahead, or when they face difficulties or failures, they take action to overcome their obstacles. As you can see in the formula *achievement = thought × action*, even if you have a great idea, if you do not take any action, there will be no success. A leader is not just a critic who only thinks, but a person who also puts his thoughts into practice. I cannot stress enough that it is necessary to formulate action plans and follow them. The experiences you get from thinking seriously, taking action, and turning thoughts into deeds, are the best self-help book you can get. Everyone has their own book of experiences within them, but whether or not they utilize it fully has great impact on their improvement as a leader.

First, think deeply and make an action plan in accordance with it. Afterward, reflect on why things did or did not go well, and what you should do next. This practice of thinking back is very important. People who are considered to be great leaders repeat this cycle of thinking deeply, taking action without worrying, and thinking deeply again. For example, Mr. Eiichi Shibusawa, who some refer to as a father of capitalism in Japan, was involved in establishing more than 500 companies in the early Meiji era, such as the Tokyo Stock Exchange, the First National Bank, Tokyo Gas, Tokio Marine and Fire Insurance, and Oji Paper. At the end of each day, he always reflected on what actions he had taken that day, the results, and what he would need to do in the future. You can learn from your experiences and thoughts and think about actions that could make things better. This is a step-by-step method and requires patience, but if you make it a habit, you will see a big effect on your Self-Leadership development. Some company business managers also reflect on their own actions by writing them down in a diary.

"Do you know a lot about yourself?"
"Do you not only think but also make an action plan and put it into practice?"
"Do you humbly reflect on your actions daily, to consider the action you should be taking next?"

4.2. *Way-of-being (TO BE) model of self-leadership*

So far I have discussed the Action (TO DO) model of Self-Leadership, but the foundation that supports this is the Way-of-Being (TO BE) model.

If we liken these models to the parts of a tree, the trunk, branches, and leaves, and fruit are the Action (TO DO) model, and the roots that support them are the Way-of-Being (TO BE) model.

The Way-of-Being (TO BE) model supports your leadership actions steadily and invisibly. Similar to a tree that needs steady roots to grow a big

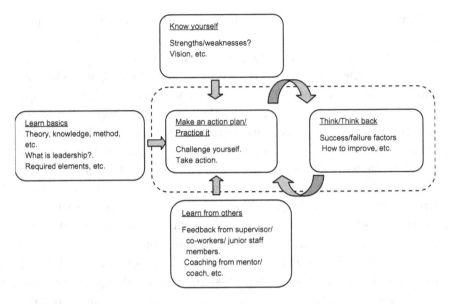

Figure 2.6.   Leadership development method

trunk, branches, leaves, and fruit, the Way-of-Being (TO BE) model is necessary for leadership as well as the Action model and is vital in creating a big vision and putting it into practice.

The TO BE (Way-of-Being) model for Self-Leadership comprises three elements:

1. Strength
2. Kindness
3. Fun

These three elements were put forth by Mr. Akira Miyahara, a business manager who served as the representative president of Fuji Xerox for six years and led tens of thousands of employees. Mr. Miyahara points out that, through his rich experiences as an employee, executive officer, and business manager, and his relationships with many political leaders, he has found these elements fundamental to the practice of being of a leader.

4.2.1. *Strength*

In the 21st century, owing to the three changes of internetization, globalization, and diversification, sometimes we cannot predict what will happen in the business environment inside or outside of a company, or whether the environment will suddenly face a great change, as in the subprime crisis that started to unravel in 2007 and the ensuing world financial and economic crises. In such an environment, a leader needs to be strong; otherwise, it is difficult to survive in business, where we face good times and bad times. Business is a competition among competitors. Just like us, other parties (other companies) will be serious contenders. This kind of situation requires that you assess your strengths accurately and maximize them. Now, how do we actualize these strengths?

In leadership, strength is not about holding power or a high position.

Mr. Kunio Nakamura, a former president of Panasonic (Matsushita Electronics at that time), led the company to a dramatic change. Although in March of 2002 they were 431 billion yen in the red, he worked on corporate revision with a strong mind and firm mission as a leader to make Panasonic rise again. After Mr. Nakamura, Mr. Otsubo became the president, and he has been accelerating further changes. One was to change the corporate name of 90 years, Matsushita, to Panasonic. He too has strong determination and skill in preparation as a leader. Also, from his business experience, Director S of NEC Group said, "A leader needs preparation. Once a person turns a necessity into a virtue [i.e. 'when life hands you lemons, make lemonade'], he will have nothing to fear."

Similarly, the strength of a leader is not about being powerful, but rather, it is about the beliefs, confidence, and preparation of the individual. These qualities will manifest in many different aspects of self-strength, which will remain stable no matter what happens in the business. Moreover, in order to master the strengths, rather than doing business for yourself and your advancement, salary, and honor, envision that you are in business for others, that is, for your customers, team, and the society. Doing so will enhance your strengths. Mr. Nakamura and Mr. Otsubo selflessly worked for the well-being of the company and society rather than act for their own gain and benefit. By pursuing the interests of public more than self, you will be able to gain true strength and confidence.

4.2.2. *Kindness*

Along with strengths, a leader must have kindness. Members will want to follow and work with a leader not only because of his strengths but also because of his kindness.

Mr. Kakutaro Kitashiro, who used to be the president of IBM Japan and led tens of thousands employees, is not only a strong leader but also kind and attentive to managers, employees, customers, relevant parties, students, and others. When I talked to him in person, I felt that his kindness reflected his true character. His kindness put him in open contact with many people. As a consequence, he received a variety of up-to-date information regarding conditions both inside and outside of the company. This helped him succeed in business at IBM. Ms. Fumiko Hayashi, who has been managing the business of BMW, Daiei, and the Nissan Group, also has strength, which is based on her strong beliefs, and kindness that enfolds her employees.

Members expect their leader to have both strengths and kindness, and they will look up to and want to follow the leader who has both qualities. In addition, when making decisions and taking action, it is important for a leader to receive a variety of up-to-date information, especially if it is bad news. A leader must be an open-minded and kind person who can accept and handle any negative information in order to make a better decision. Such strengths will help in maintaining open communication with members.

4.2.3. *Fun*

In addition to "strength" and "kindness," the third element is "fun" in business as well as in personal life.

In business, it is necessary to provide maximum value to customers, and by its nature, business imposes many difficult situations as your competitors try their best to beat you. However, masters of great leadership find fun even in a tight business situation, which allows them to concentrate and tackle problems. Although the outcome may seem bleak, such leaders will work positively, thinking "Let us give it a try, let us challenge ourselves."

The motto of Mr. Kitashiro, mentioned earlier, is "Brightly, Happily, and Positively," and he advises his employees to follow that credo in business. When introducing their ATMs (automated teller machines) in convenience stores, IBM personnel overcame many difficulties by dealing with them "brightly, happily, and positively," that is, by handling problem situations with a fun attitude. Mr. Y from IBM, who has received advice from Mr. Kitashiro, also cares about "having fun" in business. Mr. Y was in charge of a branch store that was underperforming. He coined a motto regarding having fun in the workplace. Its theme was "Since we have to do business anyway, let us do it in a fun way for world peace!" This motto was circulated throughout the store. Using this principle, within a few years he brought the store's performance from almost the lowest to the highest in IBM Japan. Mr. Miyahara says that "strength, kindness, and fun" are all important elements in leadership, but among those, fun comes first. Prof. Koichi Fuchino, guest professor at Toyo Gakuen University, has taken on the cultivation of "fun leaders" of Japan as one of his missions. He points out that it is important to feel that you are doing it for yourself and having fun doing it, instead of feeling burdened by it.

In short, if people view a situation as something fun and throw themselves into it, then it will produce strength naturally, and the kindness for others will emerge from this strength. Indeed, people who can find the meaning in doing something and can be positive in dealing with it, enjoy doing it. Moreover, no matter what kind of situation the business is in, you will be spending your life's precious moments dealing with it, so it is wise to use your time with a sense of fun, enjoyment, excitement, and sometimes even exhilaration.

4.2.4. *Correctness*

In addition to the three elements of Self-Leadership, I will add the element of "correctness."

A leader must have correctness as a human being. For example, such a person does not lie, do wrong, or cause trouble for others or society and does things that are helpful to the society. Leaders who do not care about people, or society, or its laws and conventions, might succeed for some time, but usually wind up failing in the end.

I asked Mr. Katsuhiro Utada, ex-president of Ajinomoto, "What kind of elements should a leader have?" He explained that "In a team, the No. 2 and below positions may have the best brains, but in any company or organization the person in the No. 1 [top] position must be someone who has a strong sense of propriety and justice." I believe this is indeed highly significant advice based on his experience. This means that if the top person, the one who gives out final decisions, does not have correctness, the company will fail in the end, even if it has strong management. Such companies tend to go against the society's rules or they may lose people's trust. Examples are Livedoor and the Murakami Fund, which breached the Securities and Exchange Act, and Yukijirushi, which committed mass food poisoning.

In leadership, people tend to neglect the element of correctness compared to the strength element. Nonetheless, this correctness is the foundation of the Way-of-Being (TO BE) model. In an extreme instance, a leader or member who cannot maintain such correctness should leave the business situation.

You may not be consciously aware of the influence of the *strength, kindness, and fun + correctness* equation at first, but once these elements become part of you and you can handle them naturally, you will be able to exercise very powerful Self-Leadership indeed.

Take the Way-of-Being (TO BE) model of a leader, which consists of *strength, kindness, and fun + correctness* as its base.

(1)   Set the direction by making use of your strengths and character traits (Direction).
(2)   Work hard on it (Implementation).
(3)   Learn avidly through self-study and actual practice (Learning).

Practicing Self-Leadership, as discussed in this chapter, is essential for everyone, whether or not one is a leader. Practice Self-Leadership to understand and lead yourself.

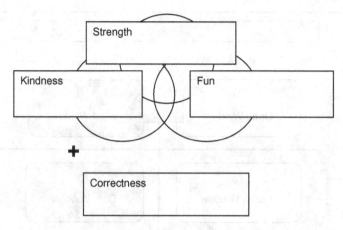

Figure 2.7. Way-of-Being (TO BE) model of Self-Leadership

▶ Why is it important to receive feedback?

Mirrors for leadership development

If you look in the mirror, you can see your body and its appearance right away. But for business, there are no mirrors. In order to increase your objective awareness of your actions, strengths, and weaknesses, it helps a lot to receive feedback from others who can see you objectively.

The Johari Window

Everyone has qualities that they know and do not know. For example, a person may be aware that he/she is dynamic and assertive. However, this person might be unaware of being, say, thoughtless regarding other people's feelings. Likewise, people are well aware of some of their character traits, but they may have some traits that they are unaware of as yet. In addition, they may only know some aspects of your character. For example, they may consider you an outgoing person. You may indeed act in such a manner, but others may not know that you are actually shy and must make an effort to be outgoing.

The Johari Window consists of four frames: the qualities of yourself that you know, qualities of yourself that you do not know, qualities of yourself that other people know, and qualities of yourself that other people do not know.

• Column ▼▼▼1

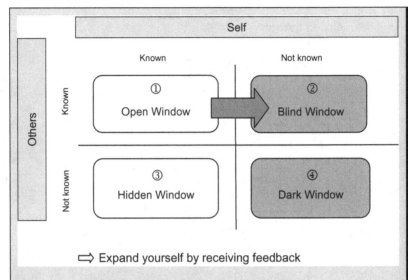

Figure 2.8. Using the Johari window

The main reason it is important to receive feedback from others is that it will help you expand what you know about yourself. You can expand the frame of the "Open Window" by increasing your awareness of qualities that you do not at present know about yourself but others do. Doing this evaluation will enable you to realize more about yourself. To quote Confucius and Socrates, by knowing more about yourself, you will be able to understand more about yourself, and this will make it easier for you to practice Self-Leadership.

▶ Find what you want to do

Moment of glory

• • •

In the Self-Leadership development training given in some companies, there is a practice called "Moment of Glory." This is a workshop in which you picture where you want to be in the business world in the future and what is the best and most glorious moment for you. In this practice, you will visualize WHEN, WHAT, WHY, and HOW in detail.

First, find a quiet place and do some deep breathing to relax. Once you are relaxed, picture how you want your future to be in 3, 5…30 years from now. Imagine the moments in which you would feel "the best" and experience "the ultimate high."

It could be anything. For example,
You are being blessed by many people for greatly expanding the business. You have succeeded in establishing a new business that you planned yourself.
You are receiving gratitude from an important customer whom you have made happy.
You are enjoying challenging yourself in business daily, with likable people. You are manifesting your abilities to the fullest extent.

In any case, picture the business moment you think is the very best, and write down the situation clearly in as much detail as possible. It is also good to talk with your friends, family, or co-workers. By talking with others, you may receive valuable feedback that helps you to realize something.

In picturing your "moment of glory," do not worry about logic or circumstances. It is possible that, in the future, obstructions may have cleared or you may be able to receive support from others to make what you imagine mostly come true. Thus you do not need to think about what you currently believe you can or cannot do, but just picture, from your heart, what you think would be the best thing that could happen.

For example, my moment of glory is when I am contributing to make Japan, Asia, and the world better through leadership development — that is, giving support to cultivate as many great people as possible by publishing books, giving lectures, and teaching at colleges and companies. My moment of glory is when I am providing my best to nurture leaders in the next generation, just like the great business expert Peter Drucker; MIT's Peter Senge, who has been contributing to the nurturing of world leaders; and world-class Japanese scholar Ikujiro Nonaka from Hitotsubashi University.

I am now doing my best to make my moment of glory come true by practicing these principles, taking action, reflecting, and learning daily. Picturing your moment of glory helps you to envision your goals. Once you do so, tell people around you about it and get their feedback or opinions. This will help you think about your vision in greater depth, which will lead to further clarification of the goal or vision required in the GROW model described earlier. These processes will help you learn what you really want to achieve and what you really want to do.

• Column ▼▼ ▼ 2

How do you take action when it is hard to do?

Many people whom I encounter are smart and good at thinking but do not take action. Therefore, I would like to emphasize the importance of "Think and Act." Both thinking and taking action are important, but if I had to choose just one, I believe the latter is more important. When I talk to people, they all come forward with good ideas, but surprisingly, many of them do not or cannot take action. Achievement is brought about by the multiplication of thoughts and actions. Even if you have a great idea, no action means no achievement.

Now, what do we do to take action? I recommend taking a little step forward first. Once you have taken the first step forward, it is easier to take the second and third steps. Conversely, once you stop to take a look around, you will only see the risks and will be afraid to take action. Therefore, I suggest that you take at least one step forward. If it is difficult for you to take action, you can ask someone to give you a supportive push. When I first started in leadership cultivation work, I was afraid to do anything because I had little experience. When I received an offer from a company to conduct a senior management class in leadership development, I was in two minds because I was not confident whether I would be able to do well. Then, my coach, Mr. O, gave me a supportive push, saying "Just take a risk and do it!" When I actually tried it, I did have some difficulties, but they were not as bad as I had feared they would be. If I had not tried conducting the class, I might never have laid the foundation for my future growth.

It is common to have things that you were afraid of before you started, but which turned out not as bad as you thought it would be, and you realized that it was good to challenge yourself. An American human resource consultant told me, "Ninety-five percent of what people are afraid of is merely their imaginations and assumptions" — and I agree. The extent to which you can challenge yourself to scale the hurdles that are high and difficult determines how much you can grow in the future. Personally, I believe that failure does not exist. Things that go well will give you confidence and make you want to attempt the next high hurdle. Conversely, things that do not go well will become ingredients for the next challenge and growth through thinking back, learning a lesson, and thinking what to do next. Therefore, in my opinion, "there are no failures in the world, just study materials — the things that did or did not go well."

First, take a step forward. Otherwise there will be no changes. Remember, no actions means no miracles.

CHAPTER 3

TEAM LEADERSHIP

1. What is Team Leadership? (WHAT)

Team Leadership is "the power to lead a team in a better direction." More specifically, it is "the power to lead a team to success and growth." In this context, "success" means improvement in the performance of the company or team, such as increased sales, profits, production output, or efficiency. "Growth" is for the individuals in a team to develop their skills. Team Leadership is the power to encourage both success and growth and to attain the team's objectives. This chapter focuses on how to acquire Team Leadership skills to lead a group.

2. Why is Team Leadership Needed? (WHY)

In a company or an organization, a team comprises several individuals. Guiding team members effectively to achieve greater visions or objectives or create value requires skill in Team Leadership. Although team members may be equipped with valuable skills, their ability to achieve good results depends on the quality of leadership. For example, in sports such as baseball and soccer, a weak team can be transformed into a great team by changing only its field manager or coach. The same applies to many companies and organizations in business. Often a company or department will undergo significant change when a new top leader, such as its president or manager, takes over. Peter Drucker, the business expert who greatly influenced Jack Welch (former CEO of General Electric) and A.G. Lafley of Procter & Gamble, also emphasizes the importance of leadership. The quality of the Team Leadership is the deciding factor governing the team's performance.

Team Leadership in the 20th century		Team Leadership in the 21st century
One-way leadership in which a specific leader made decisions and members followed them. Top-to-bottom leadership.	⇒	Leadership is more important. Leadership in every direction (top-bottom, right-left, diagonal).
It was acceptable to have visions that resemble that of other companies.	⇒	To win, visions and strategies have to be original and different from that of other companies.
People's values were similar, so it was easier to motivate them.	⇒	People's values are diversified, so it is important to motivate them in accordancewith their values.
It was important to learn individually.	⇒	In addition to individual learning, it is important to learn as a team.

Figure 3.1. Team Leadership in the 20th century versus 21st century

The business environment has changed greatly owing to the three waves of internetization, globalization, and diversification that took place in the late 1990s. Earlier, leading companies had more information than small and medium-sized enterprises or consumers, and leaders had more information or knowledge than their team members. However, due to the advent of the Internet, there is now greater access to information, depending on how effectively the Internet is used. Also, in the past, the rate of change was relatively slow, so in many cases, bosses were able to apply their knowledge and experience. But in the 21st century, changes in technologies, markets, and customers occur much more rapidly, and leaders can no longer rely solely on their individual knowledge and experience. Furthermore, there are situations in which prior experience prevents leaders from taking on new challenges. Therefore, leadership in the 21st century needs to be different from that of the 20th century.

3. The Elements of Team Leadership

3.1. *Three elements of the Action (TO DO) model for Team Leadership*

Three steps are required to exercise Team Leadership in order to lead a team to realize a vision or achieve success and create value. Here, the three elements of the Action (TO DO) model for exercising Team Leadership are discussed.

First, a team leader needs to set the direction for the team. It is important to determine the goals, standards, values, short-term objectives, and future vision of the team. Even if the team members put in their best efforts, the team will not be able to produce good results if its direction has not been set. Without a clear direction, there is a chance that all the efforts and actions of the individuals could go awry and affect the team. Hence, the starting point of Team Leadership is the setting of the team's direction.

Next, if team members do not take action, there will be no progress toward the vision or goal. Vision without action is just a "pie in the sky." Thus, action and implementation are essential. Mr. Carlos Ghosn of Nissan emphasized the importance of taking action when he made the changes needed to pull Nissan through its management crisis in 1999. He said that, in a company or an organization, as the elements of success, "visions and strategies are 5%, and the remaining 95% is taking action." That is, of course, if the visions and strategies are made explicit. After establishing the proper direction, he led the company to improve its business performance by focusing on taking action. Therefore, the ability to take action is very important. Companies and organizations will be able to achieve their goals if they formulate a suitable direction and take action.

However, by observing various companies and organizations, it is clear that another important element is involved, that is, an ability to learn. In addition to having the right direction and the ability to take action, one can learn and improve through experiencing actual achievements. This is the third important element. A capacity for learning is essential to constantly improve one's performance, make the team work better, or improve the capability of the individuals.

If the cycle of these three elements of "direction," "ability to take action," and "ability to learn" is applied effectively, the team will be able to achieve their goal or otherwise create value. This leadership cycle is based on the "VALue Model." A leadership model for creating values, its name is composed of the letters V for Vision and Value, A for Action, L for Learning, and ue for unlimited evolution. Leadership for creating value consists of the three elements of direction (setting of visions and values), action, and learning. By translating these elements into reality, one cannot

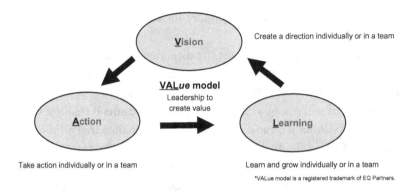

Figure 3.2. Three actions of Team Leadership: VALue model

only achieve short-term success but also build a team whose growth is continuous and permanent.

In addition, when implementing the VALue model, it is important that action be taken by the team as a whole — including the members as well as the leader — rather than the leader taking the sole initiative. In the 20th century, it was customary for a leader to assume the main role and take the initiative for creating a vision, taking action, and learning. In contrast, leadership in the 21st century is more complicated due to changes in the business environment and because past experience cannot be applied to present situations demanding leadership. In addition, human resources are now more diverse, requiring maximum utilization of the knowledge, skills, and ideas of all the members. In the past, it was thought that group unity of diverse members was best achieved when a leader led the team. However, at present, it is more important for all the team members to contribute to the leadership process. Team Leadership is about the all-member approach to leadership, in which all team members become proactive and share team leadership.

3.2. *Way-of-Being (TO BE) model of Team Leadership*

① **Strength**   ② **Kindness**   ③ **Correctness**

In Team Leadership, simultaneous with the Action (TO DO) model, it is important to apply the Way-of-Being (TO BE) model, as it becomes the foundation for supporting actions.

3.2.1. *Strength*

To survive and win in such a rapidly changing and challenging business environment, a team has to be strong. In business, there are always ups and downs. In a positive period, everything will go relatively well with any kind of leadership. But the importance of effective leadership is realized when a leader leads the team to achievements in a negative period. Even companies in such good standing, such as Toyota, Honda, SONY, and Panasonic, have experienced bankruptcy and management crises in the past. For example, Toyota had a very serious management crisis at the time of deflation in 1950. Nonetheless, they made a comeback, with assistance from the banks. Many companies or organizations have experienced setbacks. It is important to have the strength to overcome difficulties without being cowed by them. First, a leader should have a strong will and firm beliefs. Mr. Kiyoshi Seki used to work in a management position under Mr. Konosuke Matsushita and as a director of the Matsushita School of Government and Management, from which many leaders in the government and financial sectors have graduated. Mr. Seki once told me, "A leader has to have a solid will. It does not have to be a high-level one, but it is important to have a solid will." In the beginning, Mr. Konosuke Matsushita was not a strong leader because he was in delicate health and had a lackluster academic background. But he became a strong leader by having a strong belief "to make the business succeed and contribute to society."

One can build a strong team that can move forward and grow no matter what situation the business is in, by telling and sharing such strong will or belief with team members.

3.2.2. *Kindness*

Along with strength, kindness is another important element of leadership. Earlier, members of an organization were mainly permanent employees with similar values. Therefore, many of the members would usually follow the directions and orders of the leader or company policies. In contrast, teams are now composed of people of differing age, sex, nationality, and affiliation, and the way of thinking has become more diverse. In such a situation, a leader needs to motivate the members to take action by being kind towards them on an individual basis. Kenneth H. Blanchard, a leadership guru whose books (including "*The One-Minute Manager*") have sold over 10 million copies worldwide, sums up these important points about leadership into "Leadership is love." When a leader works with members with deep love and kindness, and sometimes with sternness, members will feel united with the leader and each other as a team, and they can take potential action and grow.

The way-of-being to "be strict in the conduct of business but kind to people" is an essential element in creating a strong and united team.

3.2.3. *Correctness*

In addition to strength and kindness, correctness is a necessary element. In fact, the importance of correctness (justice) in leadership was already recognized earlier but has now gained importance. In the past, problems were often concealed within the organization. Nowadays, they can be easily reported outside the company and to the mass media via the Internet. One example is the offenses against the law made by companies, such as the food labeling scandals involving Meat Hope, which sold other meat marked as beef.

World-class leadership is more than just following laws and rules and not infringing on social justice. It requires selfless consideration for the socially vulnerable, the environment, and the people. Without the right way-of-being of Team Leadership, a company may commit a serious offense or break laws and rules. As a result, it may risk the company's existence. In contrast, one example of actions that pointed out the significance of correctness is the oil fan heater incidents of Panasonic (Matsushita Electric Industrial at that time). Several people died or were injured due to problems in the manufacturing process of the heaters. At that time, under the leadership of President Mr Nakamura, Panasonic decided to adopt a right way-of-being and be a "super-honest company." They strived to keep product injuries to a minimum and changed all the advertisements and commercial messages to apologies for the fan heater incidents. At one point, they voiced their determination to visit every electronic store and customer if need be, even if it would cost a large amount of money.

Mr. S, the president of a Matsushita group company, who was in charge of the Tohoku district at that time, was determined to "find all the fan heaters at all cost." Along with his employees, he went to each sales district to search for the defective fan heaters, even during adverse weather conditions.

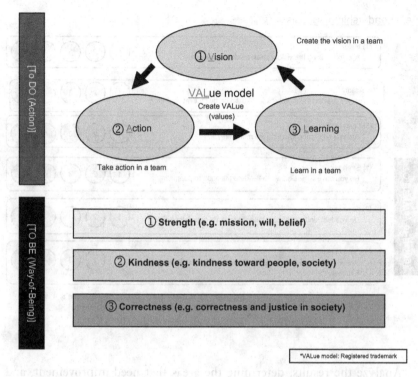

Figure 3.3. Team Leadership three actions + three ways-of-being model

Several years later, the company is still making efforts to find any problematic fan heaters that remain unfound. Correct actions such as these, based on the correct way-of-being of a team, won the trust of the consumers and society. People felt "this company is doing the right things socially." As a result, their actions had a good influence on the business.

4. Team Leadership Diagnosis

Here you can check how well you exercise Team Leadership.

Rate yourself from 1 to 5 on the following items:

① Are you able to make the vision clear to the team?
② Do you motivate the members to take action?
③ Do you cultivate/grow team members?

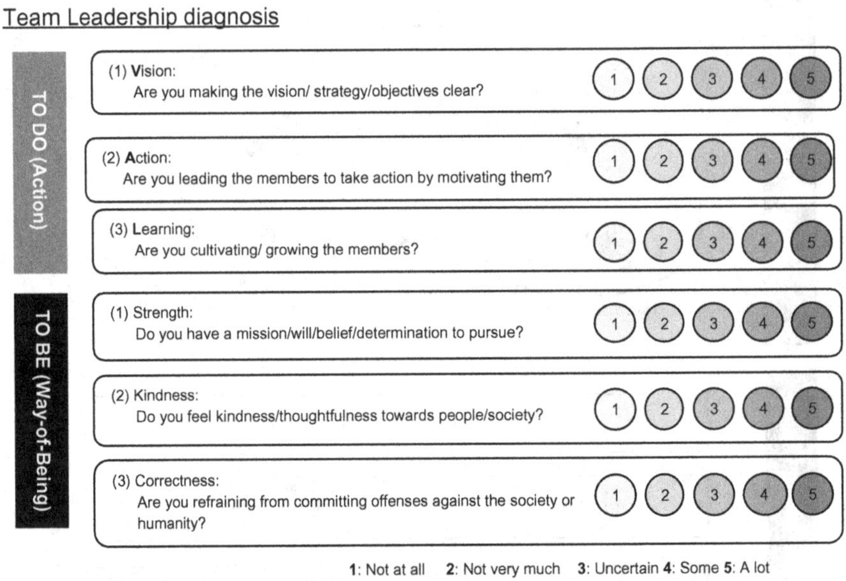

Team Leadership diagnosis

TO DO (Action)	(1) **Vision:** Are you making the vision/ strategy/objectives clear?	① ② ③ ④ ⑤
	(2) **Action:** Are you leading the members to take action by motivating them?	① ② ③ ④ ⑤
	(3) **Learning:** Are you cultivating/ growing the members?	① ② ③ ④ ⑤
TO BE (Way-of-Being)	(1) **Strength:** Do you have a mission/will/belief/determination to pursue?	① ② ③ ④ ⑤
	(2) **Kindness:** Do you feel kindness/thoughtfulness towards people/society?	① ② ③ ④ ⑤
	(3) **Correctness:** Are you refraining from committing offenses against the society or humanity?	① ② ③ ④ ⑤

1: Not at all   2: Not very much   3: Uncertain 4: Some 5: A lot

Figure 3.4.   Team Leadership diagnosis

Analyze the results, determine the areas that need improvement, and list them under "Future Actions." During self-evaluation, most people realize their strengths and weaknesses. Strengthen your present skills and improve in the areas in which you have not been able to do well. In addition to improving on your limitations, it is important to identify and work harder on improving your strengths. However, Japanese people tend to focus on their weaknesses. Peter Drucker advices "Build on top of people's strengths" and "Make weaknesses meaningless with strengths." People who are already good at certain skills, such as creating visions and strategies or cultivating human resources, should focus on improving their strengths.

5. How Do We Put Self-Leadership into Practice? (HOW): Three Actions

You can see what you need to improve, whether it is creating a vision, the ability to take action, or the ability to cultivate human resources, by doing the "Team Leadership Diagnosis." This can be used as a hint or suggestion for developing your own Team Leadership skills. Here we will look at the "making visions" process as the first step.

5.1. *Build the direction (Vision)*

The importance of "creating a vision" and "showing the vision to the team" is realized when one becomes a team leader. Although creating a vision is one of the most important functions of leadership when leading a section or a team in a major company or when managing a company, it is also one of the more difficult tasks.

The method that is being introduced here is a model based on research on how a large number of business managers and leaders create their visions. The procedure of building up a vision can be divided into three levels:

- Step 1: Present data analysis and future prediction (Considering the vision and the current situation, and predicting the future),
- Step 2: Vision-building (Creating a vision or value),
- Step 3: Vision communication (Communicating with the members about the vision).

There are two approaches to conduct these three steps: the "IQ (logical) approach" and the "EQ (emotional) approach." IQ stands for "intelligence quotient" and determining it involves taking a test in logical and mathematical thinking. Hence the IQ approach is a way of creating, analyzing, and communicating data in terms of logic or mathematics. In contrast, EQ stands for "emotional quotient," and is referred to as "the IQ of the heart." People have feelings as well as thoughts, and it is very important to take those into account.

Now we will look at the three steps mentioned earlier in terms of both the IQ and EQ approaches.

▶ **Step 1 — Present data analysis and future prediction (Perceive)**

In Step 1, an example of the IQ approach in the observation phase would be predicting the objective market data and conditions in the business world. The IQ approach is used to analyze information, such as trends and tendencies in business, the strengths of a company or department, its state of affairs, the need of the customers, and the strengths and strategies of competitors. It is important to perceive the current situation objectively and with a broad overall perspective. Moreover, analysis shows that great business managers and leaders have one thing in common: they do not rely only on an IQ approach such as objective data and analysis. They go out into the field, eager to listen to and observe their customers — for example, people from factories and at the front line of sales or young people — to understand the market and customer trends. This is an EQ approach. An example of using the EQ approach is that of Mr. Toshifumi Suzuki, who started Seven-Eleven, the largest convenience store chain in Japan. When Mr. Suzuki was in the United States, he chanced upon a little convenience store called Seven-Eleven that was open 24 hours every day. This type of operation had not yet been seen in Japan. Then he researched, seeking answers to his questions: "Why does this type of store exist? Does it make a profit? Why do customers come to the store at night?" He came to the conclusion that although there were no convenience stores in Japan at that time, this kind of business would expand as the Japanese lifestyle changed in the future. In 1975, he opened an experimental store on an all-day/ all-night basis. Customers coming to the store at night appreciated the concept. Mr. Suzuki felt intuitively "This will be a good business," and, without in-depth data or a precedent in Japan, went ahead to start the Japanese Seven-Eleven convenience store chain, which now has stores throughout the nation. Also, Mr. Masatoshi Ito, the business manager of Ito-Yokado, told me that, "Mr. Konosuke Matsushita of Matsushita Electronics was envisioning things not only in his head but with his whole body and soul. We need to think not only in our heads but with our whole bodies." This is crucial advice because most people tend to think but not act. In addition to the IQ way of observing and considering things, it is important for a leader to look at situations in an EQ way — to feel intuitively and with their hearts.

In the past, change was not rapid. Thus a company could respond to or countercheck the changes when they occurred or were about to occur, even after other companies had adopted the changes. For example, earlier, Matsushita Electronics (now Panasonic) was able to follow and countercheck its competitors by coming up with products similar to new products that other companies, such as Sony, Toshiba, and Hitachi, had already developed. This was because of their strong sales network of National Shop stores, of which Matsushita had 50,000 at one point. However, at present, the lifecycle of products has been accelerating, and if a company is not the first to introduce a new product into the market, it cannot make a profit. Moreover, consumers now have access to information and can instantly find out which company is developing a new or better product. Hence, in the 21st century, companies need to be able to predict their own market and create a new vision in order to be the first to introduce a novel product. Given this factor, Panasonic changed their business model to "launching our own products worldwide at the same time." Instead of following up on other companies by bringing out similar products, they now simultaneously introduce their best and exclusive products into the worldwide market. This has resulted in success. Thus it is vital to analyze the past and current trends as well as focus on what is to come.

Mr. I, who used to be a member of the board at Morinaga (a Japanese food and beverage company), told me that "Leadership in the 21st century is about the ability to see what you cannot see, and the ability to see the future." Because of the rapid changes in the 21st century and difficulty in predicting the future, the ability to foresee has become a key element to success. Also, Mr. I continued, "To see what you cannot see, you need to keep learning. You can bring yourself to perceive from communication with people in various positions or those with differing thoughts or viewpoints, from both inside and outside the company or industry." In addition, it is important to perceive and understand the nature of things without being trapped within the existing paradigm. To gain a different perspective, one must question existing perspectives and trends of thought and distance oneself from them, if necessary. For instance, it is useful to gain a different perspective on a current business management approach or common knowledge of a company or industry. For example, Mr. Kenichi Ohmae, a world-famous management consultant, teaches the importance of the ability to predict and plan the future, such as by imagining a living room of the future home. Imagine a living room 5 or 10 years from now and think what feature might become a future business opportunity. Use your imagination at full throttle to envisage some of the trends your business or industry might take in 3, 5, and 10 years from now. Then discuss them seriously with people who are in the know or who have out-of–the-box thinking. By doing so, you will eventually develop your ability to "see" the future. The ability to perceive the future and stay a step ahead is one of the important elements of leadership in the 21st century and will be ever more essential in years to come.

▶ Step 2 — Vision-building (Create)

After analyzing the current situation and predicting the future, the next step is creating the team vision. In the 21st century, the world is experiencing revolutionary changes due to the three factors of internetization, globalization and diversification, the extent of which could not be predicted earlier. One example is the world economic crisis that sprang from the subprime problem in the United States starting in 2007. As for the current economic crisis, Mr. Ghosn of Nissan emphasizes that we need a completely new way of conducting business as unprecedented new changes occur.

Here, we can use both the IQ approach and the EQ approach. For the former, it is effective to come up with strategies logically or use the strategy frameworks that you learn in business school programs. One important point is to utilize the strengths of our company and organization. We must scrutinize opportunities in the market and come up with a strategy that matches our strengths and the opportunity but is different from that of other companies in the field. In addition to creating a strategy that makes use of the team's strengths by the IQ way, the EQ method is also important. People have emotions and feelings. In your vision, it is important to include not only logical, numerical, and strategic elements but also dreams, values, and challenges to your spirit, things that you can work on with passion and excitement, for which you can feel a sense of responsibility. For example, consider the vision of Mr. Yoshiharu Hoshino of Hoshino Resort, who is managing the resort village Hoshinoya Karuizawa in Nagano and is trying to revive resorts, such as the ski and snowboard resorts Alfa Resort Tomamu in Hokkaido and Alts Bandai in Fukushima, in Japan. To motivate the team members, his vision is clear and challenging. It includes the IQ approach, such as attaining a customer satisfaction rating of +2.5 or more, a recurring profit margin of 20% or more, and an environmental index of 100P or more. It also includes the EQ approach, such as "to become a master of resort management."

▶ Step 3 — Vision communication (Communicate)

Even if a leader draws up a great vision or strategy, the team will not be able to work towards it if the vision is not shared with the team members. To take action, it is necessary to communicate with the team, that is, to share and go over the planned vision and strategy with all the members in the team. Here we use the IQ approach, in which you can use objective data, a number, or a graph to "see" or explain logically and systematically, together with the EQ approach, in which you explain your vision with passion. For example, Mr. Howard Schultz, CEO of Starbucks Coffee, keeps explaining to his employees about the kind of coffee shops he wants to provide to make the customers happy. Even so, he says he has not yet been able to express his vision fully to the employees and part-time workers. Jack Welch of General Electric also says, "I talk about the vision over and over, and I'm tired of it. But this is the most important role of a leader, so I have to do it." Moreover, Nissan's Carlos Ghosn showed his strong determination as a leader when reviving the management of Nissan in 1999. His extraordinary determination was made clear when he promised that if Nissan's revival plan failed, the entire management team, including him, would resign. From this statement, the employees understood the seriousness and determination of Mr. Ghosn to work toward the vision together, and it was one of the factors that helped Nissan to realize its revival plan. A vision will lead to action only when you keep telling it over and over so the rapport of the members will increase.

▶ Pursue both the IQ approach and EQ approach

In the three vision-making steps of "perceive," "create," and "communicate," the key is to mix the IQ approach and EQ approach well. However, many of the companies or teams seem to emphasize one approach over the other.

For example, visions such as "More than 10 billion yen in sales" or "Make a profit of over 10%" have only an IQ (logical/numerical) element, and "Make a great company!" or "Do our best at any cost!" have only an EQ element. The data you can analyze in the "perceive" phase is actually outdated information by the time that point is reached. In order to visualize before the data comes in, we need to use an EQ approach. Also, it is hard to motivate people to take action only by using numbers or logic.

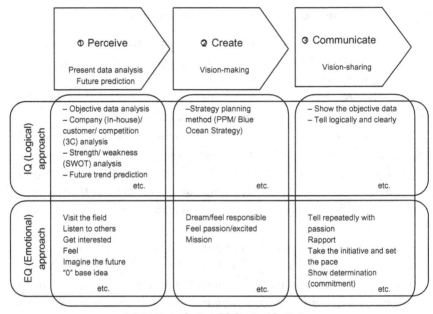

* IQ: intelligence Quotient   EQ: Emotional Quotient

Figure 3.5.   Vision-making method

Such goals will only become dry quotas. People will feel that they are doing it just because they were instructed to and will not feel much motivation to do it. They need something that excites them and catches their imagination, such as "Let us create products or services that they've never seen out there," "Let us fill the store with customers' smiles," "Let us create a store that customers appreciate all the time," or "Let us be number one in the world."

If the vision employs only the EQ approach, it will just be a daydream. It is important to use both the IQ and EQ approaches.

Mr. Eiichi Shibusawa is referred to as the father of capitalism in Japan because of his contribution to establishing over 500 companies, including the first bank, insurance company, and paper manufacturing company in Japan. He says, "In business, you need 'the Analects' and 'the abacus.'" Here "Analects" refer to the EQ elements, such as dreams, thoughts, and correctness. But a business cannot stand on that basis alone. It also needs the "abacus" calculation, that is, IQ elements such as numerical analysis of

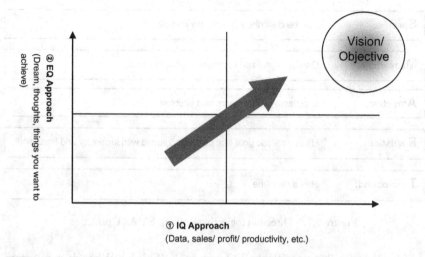

② EQ Approach
(Dream, thoughts, things you want to achieve)

Vision/
Objective

① IQ Approach
(Data, sales/ profit/ productivity, etc.)

Figure 3.6. Vision/objective to move the team. This diagram shows the philosophy of a certain worldwide management consulting company. This shows that visions or objectives, changes, and the establishment of a new business cannot be achieved with the IQ approach alone. Naturally, a consulting company is good at the IQ approach, but this emphasizes that to make a creation or change, such a company needs to follow the EQ approach as well

the business. Simply put, a team leader needs to have a strong and well-balanced approach of both IQ and EQ elements.

The "SMART principle" is a way of effectively setting a vision or objective. Its name comes from the initial letters of the five elements it requires.

Specific: The vision must be described in specifics and details.
Measurable   It must be measurable or quantifiable.
Attractive: It needs to be attractive and appealing.
Realistic: The vision must be, although challenging, achievable through your efforts.
Time-bound: There must be a time limit to achieving it.

When you create a vision, use the SMART principle as the first step.

Direction-making (vision/objective) method

Now we will create a direction (a mission, vision, value) using both the EQ and the IQ approach, referring to the above-mentioned cases.

Specific:	Can be described specifically and clearly.

Measurable:	Can be digitalized to measure achievement.

Attractive:	Is attractive to the team and yourself.

Realistic:	Has a realistic goal that can be achieved with ingenuity and hard work.

Time-bound:	Has a deadline.

Figure 3.7. Direction (objective-setting): SMART principle

First, we will start with the EQ approach. Think, "What does my team want to achieve in the future?" and "What would be its ideal shape?" As you envision, do not worry about whether you can accomplish the mission. Just think of what a great thing it would be if it happens. Next we will think using the IQ approach. Here, we digitize the EQ approach presented earlier and put it into logical form. We create a vision that has both EQ and IQ approaches by merging the IQ approach, such as deciding when exactly it should be achieved, thinking about what it will be like when digitalized, or whether we can exercise the strengths of the company or section, into the EQ approach. Now, explain the vision that you created to your team members. If the vision stays only in the leader's head and only the leader has a strong feeling toward it, it will not be shared with the team members. If the vision is shared with the team members and they resonate with it, then they will take action to achieve it. Reiterate your vision to your team members. Then, along with team members, formulate a plan of action to realize the vision and get feedback. Determine if the vision is really attractive to the team or whether they can feel a rapport with it. Create and circulate the vision by earnestly discussing it with the team members.

In the past, generally a leader created a vision and related it to the members to move them to action. In the 21st century, however, we need to come up with a unique vision that is different from that of other companies. This is accomplished by making use of team members' knowledge and soliciting their ideas. Accordingly, it is effective to create, with all the team

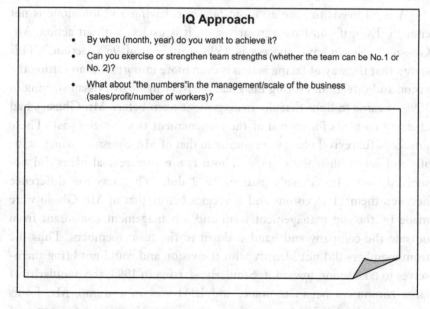

Direction-making (vision/ objective) worksheet

EQ Approach

"What does your organization/team want to achieve in the future?"

"What is your/their dream?"

"How do you want your team to be?"

"What is the value you want to hold?"

Figure 3.8.   Direction-making (vision/objective) worksheet — EQ approach

IQ Approach

- By when (month, year) do you want to achieve it?
- Can you exercise or strengthen team strengths (whether the team can be No.1 or No. 2)?
- What about "the numbers"in the management/scale of the business (sales/profit/number of workers)?

Figure 3.9.   Direction-making (vision/objective) worksheet — IQ approach

members participating, a vision that corresponds to the changes in business circumstances.

There was a manager in Toshiba whose section did not have a clear vision. Moreover, the team members had different ways of thinking and their teamwork was not good. After analyzing the situation thoroughly, he decided to conduct a "vision-making camp" — an extended session for all the team members to talk about the current vision of the team. By discussing it together in depth, the vision that had not engaged everyone fully at first became a vision that everyone embraced. Since then, the section has achieved high growth. Although the content of a vision is important, this example shows the importance of creating and sharing the vision with all the members in a team.

5.2. *Make an action plan and put it into practice (Action)* *(WHAT and WHY)*

Once the vision is created for the team to follow, the next step is to take action towards the vision. This could be represented as *Team's achievement = Vision × Ability to take action.*

A team needs to have a vision; however, having a vision alone is not enough. Even if you have a great vision, it is useless without action. Mr. Ghosn of Nissan says, success is "5% strategy and 95% action." This shows that the way of taking action is even more important than setting the vision and direction. During the great recovery made by Nissan starting in 1999, it came to light that the management team before Mr. Ghosn's had changed its plans for revival of the management twice in the past. These unsuccessful revival plans were similar to that of Mr. Ghosn — which actually did accomplish the change. Those two earlier revival plans did not succeed, but Mr. Ghosn's plan in 1999 did. What was the difference between them? The visions and strategies before that of Mr. Ghosn were made by the top management team and a management consultant from outside the company and handed down to the team members. Thus the team members did not identify with the vision and could not bring themselves to take action toward it. Similarly, starting in 1993, the popularity of large computers began to wane, and IBM was in a slump. Mr. Louis Gerstner, who led IBM to recovery, also emphasizes the importance of "taking action." At that time, IBM was good at formulating visions and strategies but fell short of expectations when taking action. Consequently, he forced all the members to channel their efforts into taking action. The former president of Toshiba, Atsutoshi Nishida, who tried to bring about change in the Japanese corporation, often used the phrase "take action" to convey to his subordinates the importance of acting on the vision of the company. In fact, although many companies and teams that I have observed create a good direction (vision), the vision remains of no practical use because the team members do not take serious or vigorous action.

Now we will look at the second element of Team Leadership — "the ability to take action."

A major company conducted an in-house survey of its headquarters and business departments and found that organizations with highly moti-vated members, irrespective of whether it was the sales, marketing, research, or production department, depend on two factors:

- Whether the vision is clear and communicated throughout the department.
- Whether there is good intercommunication between the various levels of staff members.

These factors are more significant than concerns such as the prestige of the work or having less overtime work. This tells us that coordination between vision-creating and communication will result in motivating the members and enhancing their ability to take action.

Vision × Communication = Action

Result + Feedback + Return = Continuity of the action

Two approaches for strengthening the ability of the team to take action

5.2.1. *The holistic approach for achieving the vision and goal*

This approach relates to the direction-making (vision/strategy) discussed in the previous section. It is necessary for a leader to not only have the right visions and strategies and share them with the members as information but also build a strong sense of belief and commitment in order to achieve the goal. Now, what do we have to do to share the visions or strategies and build a strong sense of belief and commitment?

- **Participation of members in the vision/strategy/action plan-making**

First, the members should participate actively in the vision/strategy/ action plan-making. Instead of the traditional top-down type of leadership, in which a leader creates a vision and the members take action, a leader should act as a facilitator and involve the members in the process. In the management of my company, I have realized that members can have difficulty in sharing and feeling a rapport with the visions or strategies that I formulated. To remedy this, we conduct a vision meeting every month, in which all the members participate in creating a vision, devising the action plan in detail, and managing the progress.

Moreover, better visions and strategies may be created if the members are involved, as they may have more knowledge about the fields, customers, and market than the leader. When the leader continually emphasizes the vision of the team, the members realize its significance and are motivated to work toward it.

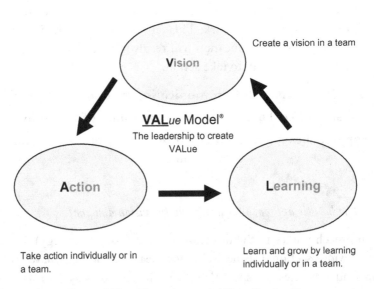

Figure 3.10.   Three elements of Team Leadership

- **Have a reward linked to attainment of the vision**

When the vision is achieved, members should get some benefit from it. Offer a reward in accordance with the achievement, such as a raise in salary or annual bonus, such as in Nissan, or awards or prizes, such as that given in Yellow Hat. Another specific and practical way is to give the team some verbal acknowledgment and appreciation, such as "You did a good job," "You made a great effort," or at least "Thank you," at the same time as giving out material rewards. In fact, leaders who have high motivation and produce good results value such nonmaterial recognition. It is important to include verbal encouragement rather than solely giving material rewards. Ms. Fumiko Hayashi, who has been a manager at BMW, Daiei, and Nissan Group, continually gives employees words of acknowledgment such as "You're doing a good job" or words of appreciation such as "Thank you" when she encounters employees who are doing well. This results in improving the motivation of the members at the company and strengthening the action-taking skills of the team.

5.2.2. *Individual approach*

▶ **Know what makes people motivated (HOW)**

Think about this: what is it that makes people motivated to take action or lose motivation? Although there are varied opinions, one thing that is certain is that the motivational factors depend on the individual. To explore that, fill out the following worksheet, "Motivational Factors." The worksheet lists 13 items, such as "Company policy and management," "Boss," "Human relationships at work," "Salary," "Sense of accomplishment," "Work itself," and "Self-development." Pick five of those items that you think are your main motivators, and rank them from 1 to 5, with 1 being the highest. Then enter the numbers in the brackets under "Yourself." Similarly, under "Member A" and "Member B," enter what you think may be the motivational factors for one or two of your junior staff members or co-workers. What you can learn here is that you and other people have different motivating factors. "Sense of accomplishment" or "Self-development" may be the motivators for some people, and "Acknowledgment from others" or "Human relationship" may do it for others. Some may find motivation in "Work itself."

You	Member A	Member B		You	Member A	Member B	
			Company policy and management				Achievement
( )	( )	( )	Supervision	( )	( )	( )	Recognition
( )	( )	( )	Relationship with supervisor and peers	( )	( )	( )	Work itself
( )	( )	( )	Work conditions	( )	( )	( )	Responsibility
( )	( )	( )	Salary	( )	( )	( )	Advancement
( )	( )	( )	Personal life	( )	( )	( )	Growth
( )	( )	( )	Status/Security				

Figure 3.11.   Motivational factors

People have different factors for motivation. One cannot assume that junior staff members or co-workers have identical motivation factors as the leaders. This means that you should use an individualized motivational approach for each person. In the worksheet shown in Fig. 3.11, we imagined the cases of two team members — for example, a junior staff member and a co-worker. But if you are doing this worksheet in a seminar at the company, you can compare your guesses with the actual answers of junior staff members or co-workers. When a major communication maker presented this worksheet at a seminar, the answers of the junior staff members were completely different from what the managers expected. In short, it turned out that those managers had been using an off-base motivational approach toward those junior staff members up until then. Therefore, naturally, there was no increase in the motivation of the junior staff members.

It is necessary to know what makes a person motivated — whether it is the "achievement," "growth," "human relationship," or "recognition." One tends to assume that the motivational factors of people are identical, but in reality, they vary from person to person. The easiest and best way to know what motivates a person is to ask the person directly. Once you know the motivational factors of other members, you will naturally know how to work with them. For members who want to feel a sense of accomplishment, give them jobs that are of high level and challenging. For those who want self-development, give them a job from which they can learn new things. For members who value being acknowledged by others, give them words of acknowledgment and appreciation such as "You're doing well," "You did a good job on this," and "Thank you." When you provide a motivational approach tailored to each person, each individual will show noticeable growth, and this will enhance your team's ability to get things done.

▶ Two types of motivational factors

According to the Herzberg theory, motivational factors can be divided into two groups. One group consists of "hygienic factors," derived from the Greek word for "health" (literally meaning "living well"). If these factors are not fulfilled, you will feel dissatisfied. The other group is called "motivational factors," which make your motivation rise according to their level of fulfillment.

In the worksheet that you filled out earlier (Fig. 3.12), the items on the left side of the list are the "hygienic" factors, which, if not fulfilled, make you feel dissatisfied. For example, you feel unhappy if the company policy is not very well thought out, your boss is not a very good leader, you have an uncomfortable human relationship at work, the work conditions are too hot or too cold, the salary is low, problems in your personal

Herzberg theory

Hygienic Factors (Dissatisfaction Factors)	Motivational Factors (Satisfaction Factors)
Things you may be dissatisfied about	Things that increase your satisfaction when fulfilled
o Company policy and administration o Supervision o Relationship with supervisor and peers o Work conditions o Salary o Personal life o Status o Security	o Achievement o Recognition o Work itself o Responsibility o Advancement o Growth

Figure 3.12.   This diagram shows the theory of Frederic Herzberg, a psychologist in the United States.

Source: "Comparison of Satisfiers and Dissatisfiers." An exhibit from *"One More Time: How Do You Motivate Employees?"* by Frederick Herzberg, January 2003

life are affecting your work adversely, or you are afraid you may get laid off at any time.

The "hygienic" factors need to be comfortable, so that people will not feel dissatisfied. But this does not guarantee that, when these hygienic factors are brought to their comfort level, their motivation will increase. An individual's motivation does not necessarily rise in proportion to the comfort of the work conditions, and often a person's motivation does not increase twofold if the salary is doubled. In contrast, when the motivational factors on the right-hand side of the figure are fulfilled, people's motivation does increase. For example, when people feel a sense of accomplishment, they will want to try hard the next time, and the time after that. People also feel motivated when they receive acknowledgment for their work, if the job is interesting, if they are given some responsibility, or when they are promoted or develop their skills. Again, the hygienic factors need to be made as comfortable as possible. Although you do focus on the hygienic factors, people's motivation does not necessarily go up, or stay high always. Hence, although the hygienic factors must be within the individual's comfort zone, at least to the minimum extent, it is also important to address the motivational factors (satisfaction factors) on the right-hand side of the figure.

When I was working in Hong Kong, I made a mistake in applying this approach. I set the starting salary for a new junior staff member, and when he saw the figure, he complained and wanted to know why his salary was so low. So the next time, when a raise was due, I gave more consideration to the salary, to ensure that it would be fair, and I prepared to explain my decision in depth. I tried to make the salary a factor in increasing his motivation. However, on that occasion, although the junior staff member's motivation did go up slightly, it did not rise as much as I thought it would. Looking back now, I see that although the junior staff member did have an actual complaint about the salary, his internal motivation also needed self-development and acknowledgment from me as a boss. Nevertheless, since I focused only on the monetary compensation, it was not enough to significantly increase his motivation.

In the same way, while still meeting the needs of the hygienic factors, a leader needs to pay more attention to the motivational factors. Furthermore, it is very important to direct your approach to the key motivation of each individual team member. The leaders and managers I meet at company seminars or consulting sessions tend to focus more on the hygienic factors, such as salary, work environment, and human relationships. Of course, these factors need to be adjusted, but people's motivation will go up if you then address the motivational factors, and this will contribute to their ability to act.

▶ **Addressing higher-level needs — Maslow's hierarchy of needs**

Another famous theory dealing with motivations is Maslow's "hierarchy of needs." This theory describes human needs in the form of a pyramid with five levels (as can be seen in Fig. 3.13.). It starts with the most basic needs as the bottom layer, and when people's needs of each level are met, they will seek the needs at the next level. The first level is that of the "physiological needs," such as eating and sleeping. Once these needs are fulfilled, the needs of the second level will emerge — that is, the "safety needs," such as living in a safe environment. When these needs are fulfilled, the person will

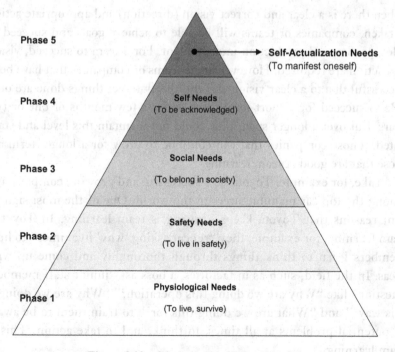

Figure 3.13. Maslow's "hierarchy of needs"

go up to the "social needs" level — the need to belong in society, the company, or a group. Once a person feels a belonging to society, "self needs" will emerge; this is the level in which people want to gain respect or acknowledgment from others in society. Then, once the self needs are fulfilled, people will go to the "self-actualization needs" level, in which they want to develop themselves or achieve something on their own.

For example, one approach to make junior staff members feel motivated toward safety needs is to use the tactic of telling them, "You will be fired if you keep doing things like this." In comparison, the approach in which you give members acknowledgment or praise targets phase 4, the self needs. The approach that makes them feel a sense of accomplishment or self-development targets phase 5, the self-actualization needs. This, then, is one leadership approach for getting things done — by motivating people through an appeal to the needs of a higher level.

5.3. *Learn from the experience (Learning)*

When there is a clear and correct vision (direction) and appropriate action is taken, companies or teams will be able to achieve goals and succeed in sales, profits, and production improvement. For a team to succeed, vision and action are required. However, some teams or companies that have been successful due to a clear vision and the ability to get things done are only able to succeed for a short term, such as for a few months or one or two years. But over a longer span, they could not maintain this level and stagnated. Those companies that can continue to grow for a longer term are those that are good at team learning.

Take, for example, Toyota — a successful and growing company and among the top car manufacturers in the world. One of the most significant reasons that Toyota keeps growing is team learning. In Toyota's team learning, for example, they "repeat asking 'why' five times" to help members learn to think things through thoroughly and come up with ideas. In the field, such as in factories, a boss asks junior staff members questions like "Why are we doing this operation?" "Why are we doing it this way?" and "What are we doing this for?" to train them to be aware of potential problems at all times, to think, and to take action. This is team learning.

Charles Darwin, in his theory of evolution, said "it is not the breeds that are strong that can survive, but those that can respond to change." For a team to respond to changes, we need team learning. Even if a team is strong at present, in today's rapidly changing society, the team will have a hard time surviving without learning and evolution. A team's constant learning will result in the making of a great vision and the taking of effective action that will build a very strong team. As another example, at General Electric, a world-class profitable company, they always think things through, individually or in a team, and learn from the process. They come up with a better vision and strategy by repeatedly employing the team learning concept, in order to put out better products and grow their system further.

Although vision-making and action-taking are essential in achieving goals, the cultivation of people is also very important in order for an organization to maintain long-term growth and its employees to grow at the same time. The business world is different today. Unlike earlier days, we cannot succeed merely by doing simple tasks or doing what other companies do. It is important to cultivate people who can create new ideas and strategies.

▶ **"Teaching" (to teach answers) and "Coaching" (to lead the person to find answers)**

There are two approaches to human resource cultivation: "Teaching" and "Coaching." In Teaching, a leader provides answers, know-how, or skills, with directions such as "Please carry out this task this way," "Please handle this customer this way," "Follow this schedule," "Please stop doing things like that because it might pose a problem." Many of the basics of business, such as how to do a job and how to handle a customer, can be taught. In contrast, Coaching is a way of leading the person to discover the answers. A leader listens to the member and asks questions to help him or her find the answers. For example, in Coaching, a leader asks questions that help the members to understand the situation and find answers on their own, such as "What do you think is a good way to do this job?" "How do you think you should handle this customer?" "What is your opinion about the schedule?" "What do you need to be careful about for this job?" Which way do you usually use to cultivate your members?

Both Teaching and Coaching have advantages and disadvantages.

▶ **Advantages and disadvantages of Teaching**

The advantage of Teaching is that you can transmit basics or rules in a short time. The disadvantage is that if this approach is overused, then members will not think or make decisions by themselves. Instead they will tend to wait for a leader to give them an answer. As a result, they may not be able to grow and may experience a lack of motivation.

The motivation level is very different when you are told to do things rather than deciding to do it yourself. People tend to have greater motivation toward things that they come up with on their own. Similarly, the disadvantages of the Teaching approach concern growth and motivation. Nevertheless, Teaching is definitely a requirement. For example, for newly recruited staff members and people who have just joined a team and do not know the basics yet, it is best to teach them starting from the basics. In addition, the Teaching approach should figure prominently in giving directions for problem situations, such as the handling of customer complaints, quality control troubles at a factory, and machine breakdowns.

▶ **Advantages and disadvantages of Coaching**

The main advantage of Coaching is that you can train the person to think on his own, which is the exact opposite of Teaching. Coaching helps cultivate independent employees and members who can take the initiative

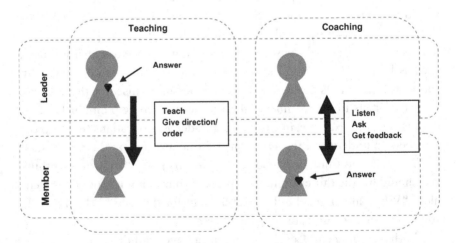

Figure 3.14. Two approaches for human resource cultivation

to think and take action. Also, members may come up with good ideas that a leader had not thought of. This is because members, being closer to the field or to customers, have more detailed and fresh information. This helps not only the members to grow but also the leaders to obtain new information and ideas to aid in their own learning and growth. Conversely, if a person does not have sufficient experience or skill, it may be hard for him/her to come up with answers. Another disadvantage is that asking questions for each issue — such as "How do you proceed with this job?" and "What about the schedule?" — takes time and is not practical in urgent situations.

▶ **Use both Teaching and Coaching, as the situation demands**

In the 20th century, when internetization, globalization, and diversification were less influential, a leader used mainly the Teaching approach, relating his experience and skills. In that era, as changes were relatively fewer and smaller, the emphasis was on prior experience. Moreover, during pre- and early-Internet days, leaders had more information, from inside and outside of the company, than the team members. But now, in the 21st century, customers, markets, and technologies have been changing dramatically owing to the three waves of change. Past experience and skills alone are no longer effective. The ideal cultivation of human resources is to use both cultivation approaches effectively, with a good understanding of their advantages and disadvantages. It is not all about Teaching versus Coaching but about using both effectively as the individual business situation or member may require. For example, using the Teaching approach, newly recruited staff members need to be thoroughly taught the basics of their jobs, company rules, and manners toward customers. Once they learn the basics, Coaching will be effective in making them think for themselves, and decide how they should handle a certain customer and how they want to conduct a presentation for the next proposal. As in other fields such as sports, martial arts, and music, in business too it is important that people learn the basics thoroughly at the beginning. Otherwise, their later growth will be notably different from that of people who learned the basics properly. After establishing a firm foundation in the basics, members can use their own ingenuity. This way, Coaching will be more effective.

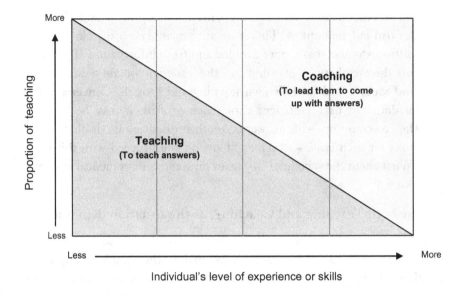

⇨
Apportion the two approaches according to the person's experience/skills.

Figure 3.15. Effective use of Teaching and Coaching

Figure 3.15 shows the use of both Teaching and Coaching. The horizontal axis shows the level of experiences or skills of a person and the vertical axis shows the proportion of Teaching used. Teaching is typically used with newly recruited staff members and new part-time workers who do not yet have much experience or skills. When they start handling their jobs — by three months, six months, or a year — the amount of Teaching they require diminishes. Then there is a concomitant increase in the proportion of Coaching, making them come up with answers themselves. Eventually, they will be able to think well on their own, without getting answers from a leader. It is a good idea to slowly increase the proportion of Coaching and adjust the Teaching/Coaching ratio according to each individual's level.

I always used to do Teaching, as I thought a leader was supposed to teach the members everything about how to do the job. As a result, the members never tried to think on their own because they assumed that all the answers should come from the leader and waited until they were given directions. Talented and motivated members lost their enthusiasm because of receiving too many directions and orders. Moreover, I did not know anything about the Coaching approach at that time, so there were times that I could not lead correctly because I myself had difficulties when I, the leader, did not know what to do.

In such cases, Coaching is a very useful approach for asking about information or ideas directly from the person. Members know more about the customers and the market and see things differently from the traditional ways. A leader can draw information or ideas from the team members. These days there are ample opportunities to conduct seminars for company business managers and directors and polish my Coaching skills. For example, when a sales department manager becomes a director, in addition to his or her specialty area — such as the sales department — he or she will have to be in charge of departments such as human resources and accounting, and in some cases technology and manufacturing departments too. In this case, having plenty of experience and skills in sales, this person can use Teaching. However, the person cannot do the same for the human resources or accounting departments. Moreover, the technology and manufacturing departments are not the individual's specialty either, so he or she cannot do Teaching. As a result, the person may face difficulties. In order to surmount this obstacle, this leader needs to do Coaching, that is, drawing opinions and ideas from people in the field, while maintaining his/her own ideas as the base. Then he/she will be able to expand the business as a director. For example, Director H of a major electronics maker used to work solely in the sales field and became a section head and manager of the sales department. Then he became a director of departments that included the factory manufacturing department. He did not have any experience in the factory manufacturing department, so he asked the employees in the field, the section head, and the manager of the department about the company's manufacturing and technologies. Then he asked questions such as "How do we need to proceed in the future?" and "What are our possible problems in the future?" He compared the answers with his own thoughts, and once he concluded that they presented no problems, he would accept their proposals. If he did find anything wrong with them, he would conduct Coaching from a different perspective to deepen the person's understanding or help them realize things so that they could bring about a better resolution. Thus he pursued his role as a director splendidly by using Coaching effectively in the fields that were not his specialty. Of course, this tactic is not limited to directors. For example, it could be used when you are promoted and are in charge of more fields of operation. Another application might be when Worker A is now responsible for tasks that Workers B and C were formerly in charge of. In this case, Workers B and C know better about the tasks they have been handling. Worker A can benefit from asking them questions through Coaching.

Instead of assuming that "a leader must teach everything," the key is to draw answers from members, without hesitation, about things you do not know and things they know better. Members will be able to gain more motivation and grow better that way. Use the Coaching approach to draw out the knowledge, experience, and information of the junior staff members. Moreover — and this should not be surprising — some junior staff members have more skills and experience than the leader. Many leaders seem to have problems applying Teaching to people whose skills and experience exceed their own. In such cases they feel awkward and under pressure. But the Coaching approach can still be used with such people. Take, for example, the man who coaches Tiger Woods, the world's top professional golfer. He is probably not as good at playing golf as Woods, but he can use Coaching with him to polish Woods' golf skills to win at a competition. The coach of Hideki Matsui, a major leaguer, is probably not as good at batting as Matsui, but he can use Coaching to help him at batting. You can say the same in business. You can use Coaching with members in the technology field even if you do not have more skill in that field than they do.

▶ After-Coaching

If the business situation is an emergency, you can use the Teaching approach to handle it immediately. For example, when there is trouble with a customer or a problem in quality control, a quick response is required at any cost; hence, use the Teaching approach. Visit the customer as soon as possible to apologize and explain or find out the cause of the quality problem right away to come up with a countermeasure. In such cases, I especially recommend an approach called After-Coaching.

For example, when a problem situation occurs, first use Teaching to tell them how to deal with it or explain it. Then, after the problem is solved, use Coaching by asking questions like "Think: why did you receive directions like those?" "How would you think and take action next time?"

"What do we need to do to prevent a problem like that happening again in the future?" If After-Coaching is conducted, members may be able to think and take action themselves when a similar issue occurs in the future. Then, in an emergency, members will be able to handle it right away themselves, without asking for directions from the leader, therefore resulting in a rapid response to the problem. In addition, members will grow and the leader need not give directions each time an emergency arises. Then the leader can spend his time on his regular assigned tasks or others. For such circumstances, After-Coaching is very effective.

When I conducted a seminar for department managers of a major electronics maker, an attendee said, "Today, almost everything in a company needs emergency handling," and "Therefore, we have to make sure to give directions right away." But if a leader teaches everything, he/she will need to do Teaching all the time. In this case, if a member were out in the field alone, he/she would not be able to make a decision, and as a result, the handling of the emergency could be delayed. In fact, at that time, the company had a rigid top-down type of leadership in which the top people made the decisions and the junior staff members followed them. Therefore, the motivation levels were very low among members and company performance was not great although it was a top company with many valuable employees. Therefore, it is important to cultivate members who can think and take action on their own, by using After-Coaching effectively.

Next, take the case of a manager at a foreign-affiliated company. She was an education-minded individual, and when her junior staff members came to ask her opinions she would spend 20 or 30 minutes, sometimes up to an hour, expounding her teachings at length and in great detail. At a glance, it seemed like a very informative approach that would better help junior staff members to grow. But one day I noticed that a junior staff member had become totally "a worker who waits for orders" and one who could not think for himself. He would come and ask her about everything because he could not make decisions on his own. Consequently, I told the manager to reduce the amount of Teaching and use mainly Coaching. I also told her to ask questions like "What do you think about it?" when her junior staff members came to her, instead of immediately teaching them answers. At first, the junior staff member was very perplexed. But when she kept asking him questions to make him think, he eventually started to develop his own opinions. Then she gave him a little pat on the back by saying, "That sounds good. Let's try it..." The junior staff member gained more confidence and regularly contributed ideas that the manager would not have come up with herself. Naturally, as junior staff members are closer to customers and the market, they have more ideas, and as a result, he became a more independent thinker.

The approach to be used — Teaching or Coaching — and its proportion depends on the leader, the members, and the business situation. But in terms of cultivating the members, if a leader uses mainly the Teaching approach, he/she can handle up to 10 members. If a team has more than 10 members, it is difficult to perform Teaching without also using the Coaching approach effectively. When a leader who habitually uses the Teaching approach changes to the Coaching approach, members may initially get confused because instead of being provided with the answers, they are being asked questions such as "What do you think?" and "What is your idea?"

According to my experience and that of many other leaders, if you apply the Coaching approach patiently for two or three months, members who used to wait for orders will stop expecting answers to be given and start thinking and taking action on their own. Eventually, they will become independent. Until then, leaders have to persist with patience. How do I use Teaching and Coaching? First, I use Coaching even with a person who has little experience or skills. I ask the members questions like "How do you think we should proceed with this project?" and "What do you think about this problem?" Even the members who do not have much experience might have done some research on their own and given thought to such questions, and might come up with their own answers. You will not discover this until you ask them questions. If they come up with answers, I keep asking questions and continue with the Coaching approach. If they cannot come up with answers, I change the approach to Teaching and tell them "Please handle it this way this time." Then, after the task is completed, I conduct After-Coaching by asking them "How did you feel about it?" "What do you think went well?" "What did not go well?" "How would you do it if you have to do it next time?" In doing so, members may be able to come up with answers themselves without the help of the leader next time. With this strategy I eventually bring the members to think and take action themselves. In fact, the approach in which you think by yourself and ask questions of yourself is called Self-Coaching. If a leader continues to conduct Coaching and After-Coaching with the members, they will start to do Self-Coaching by asking questions of themselves. Thereby, members will be able to coach themselves and become independent and grow without the leader's coaching. Then such members can coach their junior members, who in turn can become independent. This spiral of learning through Coaching is good for the team, and the team will become one that learns well.

▶ The "Trust Relationship" that becomes the foundation of Coaching

Here I will discuss Coaching in more detail. I define the Coaching approach here as "Leadership Coaching," as it employs leadership. Leadership Coaching is a communication approach for drawing out a person's capabilities as much as possible and leading them to success and growth. Needless to say, in business it is necessary for a team to achieve good results, such as increased sales and profits, and improvement in productivity and quality. Bringing a team to success in such areas is one of the key objectives in business. But in order for the team to continue to succeed, members need to grow by gaining more knowledge and improving their skills. In Team Leadership, the success of the team and the growth of its individuals must be achieved because these elements are required in order to create value continuously — not only for the short-term but also for the medium- to long-term. The objective of Leadership Coaching is to enable both the team and its individual members to have a win–win relationship, instead of a situation in which, for example, the team has scored a good achievement but the members are tired in body and mind, or the members are having a good time but the team is not doing well. The key to Leadership Coaching lies in supporting the person to come up with answers or drawing answers from them. As mentioned earlier, people have more motivation to do the things they come up with rather than the things they are told to do. Try to draw answers from the members by asking questions from different angles or by giving clues, so that they will take the initiative to take action, learn, and experience good growth. When you do so, use communication techniques such as listening closely, asking questions, and giving feedback.

But some leaders tell me, "Even when I use communication techniques, the members do not respond or talk to me from their hearts." In such a situation, I ask the leaders to check the level of the trust relationship between the leader and the members. Without a trust relationship, you cannot draw out a good answer even if you use communication techniques to ask questions, listen closely, and give feedback. Then Coaching cannot be carried out to bring success to both the team and its members. A trust relationship is very important because it is the foundation of all businesses. Stephen R. Covey, a researcher on the subject of the trust relationship, says in his book "*Speed of Trust*" that, in business, achievement is usually described as *Vision × Ability to take action*. But in an organization where people are involved, another element is added through the trust relationship.

Achievement = Vision × Ability to take action × Trust relationship

If the level of trust relationship in a team is 100%, the team members can exercise 100% of their ability. But if the level of trust relationship is 80%, the achievement will be 80% of what they should be able to do, and if it is 50%, the achievement will be 50%. We have to remember that the trust relationship is indeed an important element for a team. When I observe the organizations I have been in and the companies I have dealt with, I do notice what a great effect the trust relationship has on the teams.

How do we improve the trust relationship?

How can we build a trust relationship with the members?

I believe there are many elements involved in trust relationship, and one of them is about "having ability." For example, a leader needs to have ability as a leader so that the junior staff members will want to follow him or her. People do not trust someone who has no abilities, judgment, job skills, or communication skills. Then again, people do not trust or respect someone who is not great as a human being either, even if the person has great skills for work. People can trust someone who has a reasonable amount of ability and has understanding and consideration toward others. If a good trust relationship is not present, check which one of those two areas — ability or interpersonal communication — is the problem. If interpersonal communication skill is the problem, it is good to deepen the understanding between the leader and the members. Talk with them frankly and sincerely. You may have some disagreements, but Coaching will function well once the trust relationship is built up by deepening the understanding little by little through dialogue and asking each other questions.

▶ Team-Learning: Creative Dialogue (Creative learning approach)

Now that we have examined the Teaching and Coaching approaches, I will present the "Creative Dialogue" approach as a learning technique of the 21st century. Both the Teaching and the Coaching approach serve to draw out answers from either party; that is, in Teaching a leader teaches the members answers, and in Coaching a leader draws out answers from the members. In contrast, the Creative Dialogue is an approach for learning by putting ideas from both parties together. In the Creative Dialogue, both the leader and the members think, discuss, and stimulate each other to create something new. Even if neither of them seems to have answers, a new solution can be found by indulging in creative talk. The key to the Creative Dialogue is that the vision has to be shared between both leader and members, such as to become number one in the business field, create a one-of-a-kind product, or become an organization that makes more people happy. This is the first key point.

The second key point is to talk openly and honestly. It is important, as much as possible, to talk honestly about things you feel and think, and openly about information that is useful for achieving the vision — instead of feeling that you should not be saying something or that you should not talk about this openly. (The exception would be things that are confidential or that reveal company problems.) Then the other party will respond to you openly. By doing this over and over, you will be able to create something extraordinary.

The third key point is to be positive. Have a positive attitude toward things, such as "We have this problem, so let us tackle it and get it over with," and "We can make it better by doing it this way," instead of thinking that it is too difficult and impossible from the beginning.

Having a shared vision, talking openly, and being positive are the three important points of the Creative Dialogue. Good learning comes from situations where ideas and knowledge are called forth from both parties by talking about the experiences and thoughts of yourself and other people.

Moreover, when you hear the word "learning," many of you may form a mental picture of someone studying books at a desk. But in business, learning is about practicing something to gain experience in it.

You can achieve the Creative Dialogue and learn things of real value by repeating the learning and practicing techniques. Thus, it is important to properly repeat the thinking process and practice the techniques in earnest. The basics are about repeating the learning and practicing, that is, to create visions, take action, and learn. In addition, it is important to think back, or reflect on the past, by considering why something did not go well or what must be done next time. This is needed in order to move forward. Any business topic can become good learning material. A professor has pointed out that there is a pattern in the minds of great business entrepreneurs and scientists in that they observe and think deeply, discuss openly, take action nimbly and quickly, and if things do not go well, they start over again. Even Edison said that he had 99 failures and one success in 100 tries, and that it

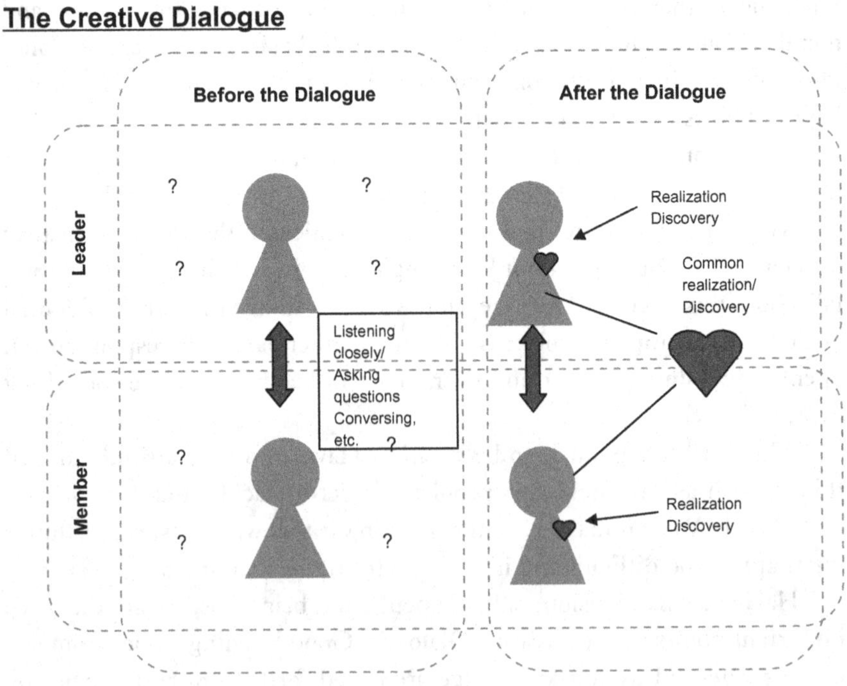

The Creative Dialogue

Figure 3.16. The Creative Dialogue

is all about repeatedly reviewing one's thoughts and taking action. You must see things deeply, think, and take action according to the natural flow. Repeating this cycle is the most important part of the Creative Dialogue. Moreover, it is important in Team Learning to not have fixed ideas such as "Business is always like that" and "This product is always like that." The key to the Creative Dialogue is to have an open mind. For example, if people were fixed on an idea that a cell phone is just for making and receiving phone calls, new services such as i-mode and the mobile wallet electronic payment application would never have been created. If people were fixed on an idea that a cell phone and a digital camera are completely different things, there would never have been a cell phone with a camera. For the Creative Dialogue, it is necessary to see beyond preconceived ideas and paradigms.

Mr. Konosuke Matsushita valued the word "honest." He gave a poster talk to managers of companies of the Panasonic group, in which he wrote the word "honest" on the poster. Having an "honest mind" means you see things without being limited by common knowledge, think deeply, and discuss, in order to create something new. What Mr. Matsushita means by having an honest mind is pretty much the same as having no fixed ideas. Needless to say, this is a very important point for a leader to learn. One of the vital elements for a leader is to have an ability to learn and to make the members learn. The objective of learning is to learn about learning. A great leader tries to learn from anything. Every time a great leader meets someone, such a person would try to learn greedily — even from people who are younger and have less experience. For example, I observed Mr. Takuya Goto, an ex-chairperson of Kao Cosmetics, at a seminar for business managers. At the seminar, he sat in one of the front rows of the conference room and listened intently to the lecture of a business manager who was more than 20 years younger, and took notes. I was deeply impressed that a business manager of a major company such as Kao was trying to learn with humility from a business manager younger than him.

As discussed in Chapter 1, in the 21st century it is more difficult to find answers than it was in the 20th century, owing to the effects of internetization, globalization, and diversification. This trend will accelerate in the future. When neither the leader nor the members have answers, using the Creative Dialogue is one way to find the best answer.

▶ Discussion and dialogue

One may, when hearing the terms "dialogue" and "argument," picture a discussion, but I recommend the "Creative Dialogue" instead. I learned about this technique at a workshop for business managers and leaders conducted by Mr. Peter Senge of MIT, who is a promoter of a learning organization, and it led me to a big realization. The term "discussion" in the original Latin had the meaning of "to pound down," and a discussion was seen as a way to solve problems by breaking them down into small pieces. In comparison, in the term "dialogue," "dia" had the meaning of "through or across" and "logos" was "meaning," in Greek. Hence, "dialogue" means "through meaning" — to talk with an open mind, think, and come to some realizations. Compare this to a "discussion," in which the objective is to draw out answers, not necessarily to come to a single conclusion. People can discover different new answers, such as "I hadn't realized it, but there actually is such a way," and "Maybe I can do it that way myself." The dialogue approach includes realizations and reflections of the individuals. The dialogue approach is not popular among organizations in Japan. It seems that Japanese prefer to find a single, firm, clear answer or conclusion. When neither the boss nor the junior staff members have answers, bring out ideas to each other openly, such as "Maybe we can think about it this way" or "How about doing it this way?" An effective way is to use the Creative Dialogue, in which everyone talks about their ideas and little by little they come up with a creative idea.

6. Three Functions a Business Person Must Apply (Roles): Leadership/Managership/Playership

6.1. *Leadership and managership*

Let us first look at leadership and managership.

To put it simply, leadership is the ability to create and bring about changes, and managership is the ability to manage others. Here, I define leadership as creating a new business or making changes in an existing business, and managership as managing and supervising things that are newly created or altered. For example, leadership establishes a new business or makes changes in the organization when the company or organization is not doing well. In comparison, managership manages and operates the newly established business effectively and efficiently. Both leadership and managership are required for companies and organizations, but it is important to use both of them effectively according to the particular business situation. Leadership is used when establishing a new thing or pursuing a change, so in some cases it requires some risks or ventures. An example of this is when Louis Gerstner of IBM changed the direction of the business from a hardware operation, which dealt mainly with large computers, to a solutions business. Moreover, since leadership is used to start a new thing or make a change, there is thus a need to picture the new vision or modifications scheme. That is, there is a need for building a vision or strategy. It is also important to make it clear why the particular vision is taken and what needs to be done within the team. In comparison, managership is used to conduct, manage, and improve things. This is not about risk-taking but about risk-avoidance. Leadership requires a medium- to long-term perspective, whereas managership calls for a short-term perspective. It depends on the business system, role, and situation you are in. At any rate, managership looks at things in relatively short spans of, say, one, three, or six months. In comparison, leadership looks at things in a longer span — 1, 3, 5, or 10 years, and even 30 to 50 years later in some cases — to create visions and strategies.

In addition, in managership, appropriate rules, plans, preparations, and schedules are required in order to take action. Once "what we are doing" and "why we are doing it" has been decided by leadership, in managership you will decide "how we are going to do it efficiently and effectively." Between leadership and managership, one cannot determine which is better and which is worse. To give an example in sports, in baseball, batting is leadership and fielding is managership. Just as both batting and fielding are necessary, both leadership and managership need to be functioning in balance in order for the team to bring achievements and growth. Figure 3.17 shows the relationship of such balance and growth of the company, with leadership on the vertical axis and managership on the horizontal axis.

A company that is weak in both leadership and managership is an "undeveloped company." Such a company will not be able to start up well or will have difficulty surviving because they cannot compete with other companies. A company that has strong leadership but weak managership is

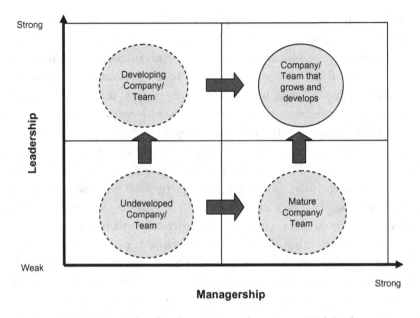

Figure 3.17.   The teams in a company that can grow and develop

a "developing company," and you can see this at the beginning of venture companies. These are organizations in which the entrepreneur produces a strong vision and strategy and all the employees take action to achieve it. However, as the venture company becomes bigger and the number of workers increases to 100, 300, 500, or 1000 workers, it cannot keep going on leadership alone. The ability to manage — that is, managership — needs to be strengthened. Otherwise there will be mistakes made in the organization's management, troubles in communication, problems in compliance with laws and regulations, and problems that may affect the existence of the team. For a company to keep going and develop, its managership needs to be strengthened. Once both leadership and managership are strengthened, the company will become one that grows and develops.

An organization that has a strong managership but a weak leadership is a "mature company," and this applies to the typical major companies. A company that has large numbers of workers typically has strong managership in management and supervision. But there are cases in which its leadership becomes weak in creating new things and making changes. If the ability to create and make changes declines, the company will go into a period of decline. Hence, such an organization needs to strengthen its leadership capacity to make changes.

Until 2000, Panasonic had a very strong management and supervision — that is, managership — but the ability to create new things was weak. But in 2001, to destroy past constraints and bad customs and create new things, its president Kunio Nakamura brought out a concept of "Destruction and Creation" that changed everything except the management policy. In the past, Panasonic had multiple departments — a department for televisions, one for audio products, another for air conditioners, and so on. Each department managed its business separately. As a result, communication between those departments was not good and a departmental rivalry existed. Thus the departments could not generate much synergy with each other, and this was not a style suitable for modern times. In this case, the company became one that grew and developed once again by doing away with the department system and reviewing the system of the National Shops stores. This is an example of an organization with too-strong managership that strengthened its leadership and made changes to revive itself. Likewise, it is important to strengthen leadership and managership according to one's current situation.

The ideal situation is one in which everyone has both great leadership and great managership skills. But in the real world, it is impossible for everyone to be good at everything. People have their strengths and weaknesses. Hence, I would like to recommend the "Co-Leadership" approach. Some people may be good at leadership and others at managership. Leadership, which seeks to take risks and start new things, and managership, which seeks to avoid risks and to manage them, are close, but not the same. It is difficult to exercise them both perfectly. If you are good at leadership but not too good at managership, in some cases it is good to leave managership to someone who is good at it. For example, Mr. Soichiro Honda, the founder of Honda, is a genius engineer and possesses strong leadership. Challenging himself to come up with new things, he created a new motorcycle and a car like no one had ever seen before, which became number one in the world. However, he is not particularly good at management and accounting. Mr. Takeo Fujisawa, who is said to be Mr. Honda's great co-head of the company, is good at managership.

With those two sharing the burden of leadership and managership, each doing what he does best, and exercising excellent Co-Leadership, Honda Motors was able to experience substantial growth in its startup and growth periods. But there is a disadvantage to the one-man style of leadership, in which a single individual exercises strong leadership. That is that the team will suffer a great drop in power after that particular individual leaves the team. A typical example is the case of Mr. Isao Nakauchi, the founder of Daiei, which grew under his strong leadership. But in later years, the company could not manage its business independently; mistakes were made in business decisions, and no successors were cultivated.

Co-Leadership works effectively for a company, or even for smaller units, such as departments, sections, or small teams. Some people are good at leadership but not as good at managership, and some are good at managership but not as good at leadership. It is important to understand your strengths and weaknesses and the current situation of the organization to determine whether to share the leadership and managership or leave it in someone else's hands. Recently, in the West, it is been pointed out that Western companies have too much managership and too little leadership (an organization's management ability is too strong and its ability to make changes is weak). Hence a great effort is being put into leadership development. Japanese people are relatively earnest and perfectionists and so are good at managing things properly. Thus, we tend to have a stronger managership than leadership. But with the business environment changing so rapidly these days, changes or new policies are required. Now more than ever, leadership is expected along with managership. Figure 3.18 shows the relationship of leadership and managership to company development in a different format.

Companies and organizations have phases of development. Growth development phases are divided into the "initial" period, in which the business has just started; the "growth" period, in which the company is expanding; the "mature" period, in which the company becomes stable; and the "change" period, in which the company needs some changes or alterations after reaching maturity. Depending on which phase the company is in, there is a need to strengthen leadership or managership. When the company has just started, the initial period requires strong leadership

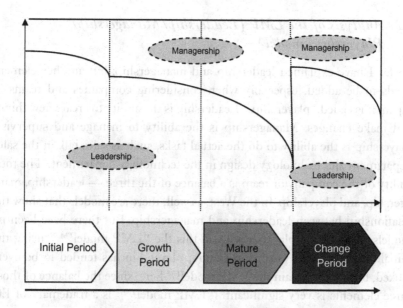

Growth/development phases of a company

Figure 3.18. Leadership and managership vis-à-vis company/organization development phases

to create a vision. Then, as the company becomes larger, managership needs to be strengthened, since more management and supervision are required and mistakes need to be avoided at any cost. But if over-managership is present, the ability to make changes will be weak. In such a case, as with Nissan and Panasonic, strong leadership must be exerted to bring about needed changes.

This is true in companies and departments as well. For example, leadership is required when a new project is started, and managership needs to be strengthened when the project is going well. Then leadership is required again when starting a new project or bringing about major changes to the current project. Which organizational development phase is your company or team in nowadays? Is it in the period of initial startup, growth, maturity, or change? Depending on the developmental phase, you can determine which effort needs to be strengthened — leadership or managership. Thus, you need to take a good look at the situation your team is in, so that you will know what to do.

6.2. *Analysis of the LMP (Leadership/Managership/ Playership) model*™

So far I have explained leadership and managership, but another element needs to be added, especially when considering companies and teams in Japan; it is called "playership." Leadership is the ability to create new things and make changes. Managership is the ability to manage and supervise. Playership is the ability to do the actual tasks, such as sales talk in the sales department and technology design in the technology department. The total ability of the company or team is a balance of the three — leadership, managership, and playership. In the West, as well, there are models that show the relationship between leadership and managership. But there have been no models that include playership. I call this the "LMP model™," using the initial letters of each word. Up to now, playership has tended to be overlooked, but I will explain the LMP model™ here, since the balance of those three elements is very significant. ("LMP model™" is a trademark of EQ Partners.)

Corporate downsizing necessitated by the worldwide economic downturn has changed the functions of some company executives. In Japanese companies in particular, I notice more people acting as the playing manager, doing the actual tasks and management/supervision at the same time, and also as the playing leader, going ahead with making the needed changes — in effect, playing double roles of leader and manager as needed.

More than 80% of the managers and leaders in Japan are playing managers or playing leaders — that is, they also perform the playing function. To give an example in baseball, when Mr. Atsuya Furuta was working for the Yakult Swallows; he acted as both manager and player. He was the

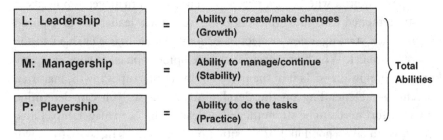

Figure 3.19.   LMP (Leadership/Managership/Playership) model™

manager, but at the same time he was also a catcher and hitter. Being a catcher and hitter is being the player, whereas being the manager is about leadership and managership. Similarly in companies, there are people who perform both roles. In the past, in the sales department, for example, junior staff members would basically be responsible for customers and products in the actual sales activities, and the manager would use managership mainly in managing the objectives and achievements of the junior staff members, and cultivating them. However, these days more people who are in the manager class and responsible for management and supervision, are acting as playing managers by having their own customers and products that they are responsible for. They perform the sales activities (the "playing") at the same time as exercising managership such as managing and cultivating the junior staff members. They have to "play" (such as performing a sales activity) and exercise leadership and managership for the junior staff members at the same time. Nowadays the playing managers tend to focus and expend more effort on their own actions, as they are also required to achieve as one of the players. This is due to the popularity of the achievement-oriented ideology. As a result, in many cases, especially in Japanese companies, there is a weakening of both leadership for creating visions for changes and managership for managing and cultivating junior staff members. This is a very big problem for many of the companies and teams in Japan.

There are external and internal causes for playing managers focusing too much on playing. The external cause is when playing managers do not have enough junior staff members to act as players. This could be a result of corporate downsizing, or a situation in which the skills of the junior staff members are as yet insufficient to trust them with the responsibility of doing the tasks. The internal cause is when playing managers are busy doing their part in the playing, or when it is easier for them to do it themselves, or simply because they are good at it. For example, sales managers who are good at performing sales operations, or managers of research and development departments who are good at or enjoy doing research themselves, tend to become playing managers. In the short term, this will result in a rise in sales, when a manager who is good at sales operations actually performs the sales operations, or advances in product development, when a manager who is good at research does the researching. However, in the medium to long term, excessive playership can cause the leadership and managership in the team to become weak. The team will have problems, such as losing sight of their vision; the management skills will become weak; mistakes will occur; or the members will show little growth. Hence, instead of putting all his or her effort into playership, even a playing manager needs to think about the balance of the three LMP elements.

Many of you may feel that you are good at playing, and that it is easier to play. I myself prefer conducting a consulting service for companies or giving a lecture as a human resource development consultant or lecturer. Nonetheless, I cannot make a team that can keep developing and growing without creating visions for the team and managing and cultivating the members. Moreover, companies in Japan usually choose, for managers and leaders, people who have been doing well as players. However, the people who are good at playing often prefer being players. A team does not grow or develop if there is no leadership or managership. Therefore, people who are good at leadership and managership should focus on those roles rather than on playership. For example, Louis Gerstner, who rebuilt IBM from its crisis in the 1990s, formerly worked for American Express, a credit card company, and Nabisco, a maker of cookies and snacks — which were not computer-related companies. Consequently, he probably did not possess a strong playership ability in computer-related businesses. However, he did have excellent leadership and managership skills, which he had learned at American Express and Nabisco, and he exercised those skills to the fullest extent in rebuilding IBM.

What you need to understand is that playership, leadership, and managership differ, that people have different strengths, different business situations will require different skills, and organizations need to use people who have good skills in the right job. A certain project manager at NEC, a major computer company, does not have very much experience or skills in computer technology or system development. All the same, she does have great managership skill, and she does a great job as a project manager by exercising such skill. If a leader or manager needed to have full experience in a certain field or master a technology, only people who can do everything could be a leader or manager. However, there are few such people. I recommend that you discover what you are good at — playership, managership, or leadership — and what the organization needs to effectively utilize each person's strength.

- The total skill of an organization is *"Each skill level × Time allocation"*

The following figure shows the LMP™ model in detail. Leadership, managership, and playership are depicted as the multiplication of the level of skill for each approach, and the resource (here, "time"). The amount of time allotted to each skill is significant. For example, if a person possesses leadership skill but does not allocate time to actually use it, no leadership will be exercised. Similarly, if no time is allotted for managership, there will be no managership; hence, managership is zero. In sum, the total skill of a team is the totaling of the amount of each skill that the team leader spends in interacting with each member.

It is important to examine carefully whether the required skill and the current situation match or a gap exists between them. For example, one way of analyzing to determine the required skills is to use a five-level index (with 5 being highest). For example, the department you are in might require a leadership level of 5, but a managership level of 4, and a playership level of only 3.

Here is another way to analyze the time allocation. Think of the total time spent on business matters as 100 and consider the proportionate time spent using each skill. For example, someone's ideal time allocation for leadership might be 30%, with 30% for managership, and 40% for playership. But in reality he only spends 20% on leadership and 10% on

Total skill of a team = Leadership ×Managership × Playership

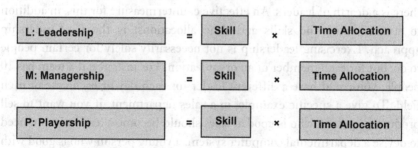

Figure 3.20. LMP™ (Leadership/Managership/Playership) model

managership, but 70% on playership. This reveals that the person is focusing too much on playership and not enough on leadership and managership.

In one study I conducted at companies, I focused particularly on playing managers. On checking the proportion of each skill in the five levels, I found that more than 80% of the people spent less time using leadership skills than their ideal time allocation. Moreover, more than 80% of them spent more time in playership than the ideal. In both skill and time allocation aspects, many companies and teams showed not enough leadership and managership but too much playership. As a result of poor in-house management, there are many examples of Japanese companies and organizations that cannot come up with a new vision, make changes, or start a new business. Additionally, in-house information or customer information may be leaked, social problems may occur, or they may make mistakes as an organization. As a countermeasure for such situations, teams or individuals should be required not to focus too much on playership but to strengthen their leadership and managership skills and resource allocations.

In the 1990s, Japanese companies had too many middle-level managers. In those days, many Japanese companies shifted those managers to playing manager positions. But now, instead of a large organization trying to work as a whole, the organizational units are smaller, comprising small teams of 10 to 20 people. This is said to be effective in helping the members of those small teams interact with each other. Each of the small teams requires a leader, but there are definitely not enough leaders. In addition, in the past, when business situations changed slowly, the top person in a big organization decided everything and people just had to follow his decisions. To respond to today's rapidly changing conditions, small teams need to move quickly, with each team under the guidance of its own leader. But again, there is a dearth of leaders. An effective countermeasure for this, in addition to strengthening the skills and time allocations, is the Co-Leadership approach. Exercising leadership is not necessarily solely for certain people to do, but for each member of an organization. For instance, if a team has 10 people, you could have a different leader for each day or each case or each field. To give a specific example, in a sales department, if you want to sell products, a person who is good at sales should become a leader. If you need to devise a departmental computer system, a young person who is good with computers should share leadership. This is an approach in which everyone can get a chance to exercise his individual capacity for leadership. It would be possible to have a different leader on a daily basis, just like a winning pro sports team that deploys players depending on the individual game's nature. To get a picture of what you need to do for countermeasures, write down the required skills and ideal resource (time) allocation and the current situation for each approach — leadership, managership, and playership. Once you do that, many of you will notice that you have too much playership. The countermeasures depend on the causes. For example, some people do not, or think that they cannot, delegate tasks to other people, preferring to do it themselves. Such a person will benefit by learning to leave these tasks to other people, or, if there is no one else who can handle the tasks, design and apply a plan to cultivate someone who can. This will cut down on the amount of playership. Moreover, trying to do something that you are not good at is more time-consuming. Hence it is good to leave that task to a competent person. If a person who is not good at computers tries to create documents on a computer or a person who is not good at managing tries to manage things, it takes too much time and is not efficient. Many Japanese people do not delegate jobs to junior staff members or other people. They tend to be perfectionists, feeling that they cannot leave such tasks to someone else, who they believe would not do them as well as they themselves would. Even if the person is not perfect for the task, it is important to feel as Mr. Konosuke Matsushita has said: "Leave the job to the person if you think he could do it 60% to 70%." Otherwise, you will never be able to leave tasks to others. Even if you try to do everything on your own, you can only succeed in doing one person's worth of sales or one person's worth of research. There's a limit to the things that you can do on your own.

If the proportion of playership becomes high, leadership and managership essentially become weak. It is very difficult to perform two roles at the same time, so a careful allocation of time is necessary. If time allocation is not applied, you will have to focus on playership because the tasks of playership are more urgent. But if you defer tasks to the medium to long term, you will fall into a vicious cycle, spending more and more time as a player. To prevent this, you need to establish your ideal time allocations and check your compliance occasionally. It is easy to monitor them if you designate time proportions for leadership, managership, and playership and enter them in your diary to look back on later. When I do this, I realize that I spend more time on playership and less time on leadership than the ideal situation. The LMP™ model can be applied to analyzing allocations for not only an individual but also an organization. You can analyze which style — leadership, managership, or playership — is required now and how each is allocated to individuals in an organization. If you do so, you will be able to monitor their proportion in the team. For example, if the proportion of managership is too high, you can make more time for leadership intentionally or, in some cases, bring in someone who is good at leadership from a different department. If the amount of playership is too high, you can give more time to leadership and managership and reduce the time allotted for playership. You can create a team that can be led to success and growth by having an effective balance of leadership, managership, and playership, according to the situation.

[4] Check the skills required for each level

When an organization is divided into three levels i.e. executive management, managers, and employees, different skills are required for each. Here an effective way of thinking called the Kats model, developed by Prof. Robert Kats of Harvard University, is presented.

In the Kats model, the skills required in business are divided into three categories: technical skill, human skill, and conceptual skill. An example of technical skill in the sales field, for example, might be in the activity of selling products to customers. For people in the manufacturing field it might be product manufacturing and assembly at the factory. In quality control, it might be inspection. Those are typical skills for actual jobs in the business world. Business also requires human communication with customers, bosses, junior staff members, and co-workers. This communication or the skill for human resource cultivation is called human skill. The third skill — conceptual skill — is required especially by upper-level people such as management executives. This skill involves ways of thinking, such as analyzing the business environment, creating a vision or strategy for the department, and detecting and solving problems.

According to the Kats model, people at the employee level especially need technical skill. They also need human skill, as they deal with customers and work as a team with co-workers. But their need for conceptual skill is still low. People at the manager level who have junior staff members under them require human skill more than technical skill because they need to communicate with the junior staff members, cultivate the personnel, and form teams. In addition, they need to have more conceptual skill than those at the employee level in order to monitor the condition of the team and

• Column ▼▼▼ 4

• Column ▼▼▼ 4

detect problems as a manager. As the level goes upward to the management executive level, the need for technical skill goes down. Human skill remains as important as at the manager level; what becomes most significant, however, is conceptual skill. This skill is very important to the executive level managers because they need to determine the vision and strategy of the company by analyzing the business environment, predicting future changes, and assessing the company's strengths and weaknesses.

It is important to strike a good balance between these three business skills — technical, human, and conceptual — by taking a look at the level you are in right now. For example, if you are at the employee level, you need to develop technical skill first, while you may strengthen your human skill over time. If you are at the manager level, skill in communication with a team and cultivation of human resources are required, since you need to get the junior staff members, co-workers, and teams to carry out work. If you are in the management executive level, conceptual skill becomes more important.

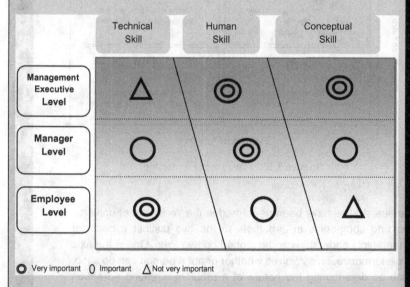

Figure 3.21. Three skills required for each organizational level and their importance levels

Source: Adapted from Robert Kats Model of Harvard University

Determine which of your skills are strong enough and which skills you need to develop further and strengthen them. This is how you use the Kats model. In many companies, there are cases in which managers have enough technical skill but not enough human skill. Many managers have little communication with others, cannot delegate tasks, or cannot cultivate people. Moreover, management executives may focus on technical and human skills and be weak in conceptual skill for creating visions and strategies. It is crucial that you fully understand which position you are in, what is required of you, what the current situation is, and what you need to strengthen in order to take action.

● Column ▼▼▼4

[5] Two axes of leadership

Effective leadership = Performance function × Maintenance function

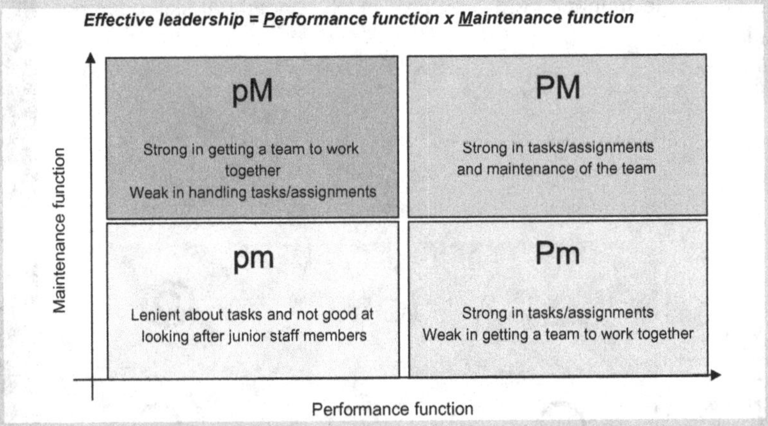

● Column ▼▼▼5

Effective leadership = <u>P</u>erformance function x <u>M</u>aintenance function

pM Strong in getting a team to work together Weak in handling tasks/assignments	**PM** Strong in tasks/assignments and maintenance of the team
pm Lenient about tasks and not good at looking after junior staff members	**Pm** Strong in tasks/assignments Weak in getting a team to work together

Maintenance function (vertical axis) — Performance function (horizontal axis)

Figure 3.22.　Two axes of leadership

Source: PM Theory by Jyuji Misumi

Various studies have been performed in the West and at universities and companies in Japan as to the two distinct aspects of leadership. Leadership can be plotted on two axes. One is the axis of performance. This involves whether or not a person can do a job, such as determining the nature of a problem, creating an action plan, solving problems, and making plans. This is called the performance function. In short, this axis shows whether or not this person can do the job properly.

When you exercise Team Leadership, in addition to your personal performance skills you will need a maintenance function for interpersonal matters such as cultivating people and having others do tasks. The maintenance function is about communicating with others, getting people motivated, and helping them grow.

When those two axes — the performance function and the maintenance function — mesh well, you can exercise effective Team Leadership because you can do the job (perform well) and have the interpersonal skills (move or deploy people well). A leader who is low in the performance and maintenance functions is immature as a leader (the "pm" box in Fig. 3.22). Also, people who are strong in the performance function but weak in the maintenance function (the "Pm" box) can perform tasks but cannot delegate tasks to others or tend to act on their own. Such individuals need to strengthen their maintenance skills. Instead of doing tasks on your own, you need to strengthen your leadership as you consider other people's feelings, give directions to others, and cultivate people. Conversely, some people are good at the maintenance function but not so good at detecting or solving problems in the work (the pM box in the figure). Although they are nice, kind, and considerate, they are not good at doing their jobs. They need to strengthen their skills for discovering problems and solving them. In any case, to exercise good leadership, both performance function and maintenance function must be strengthened. Analyze your balance of those two functions and determine your strengths and areas that need improvement. Some people may think that their individual jobs require only the performance function, but this approach will not work when a team is involved. Especially, people in technological fields tend to be that way. A technician may be able to do research alone, but if you want to work with a team you will need skill in the maintenance function.

▶ Make use of Co-Leadership

Ideally one should rank high in both the performance axis and the maintenance axis, but sometimes it is difficult to strengthen both. For example, a person who has been an engineer for a long time measures high on the performance axis but not on the maintenance axis. In comparison, a person who has been working in the human resource field may be high on the maintenance axis but low in the performance function. In such cases, it is necessary to strengthen the individual's weak area as much as possible. But Co-Leadership, in which two or more people share leadership, can be one solution. With Co-Leadership, once you know your strengths and weaknesses, you can handle leadership in the areas in which you excel, and you can get help from junior staff members and co-workers around you for the things you do less well.

If you are high on the performance axis but low on the maintenance axis, you can have as a partner a junior staff member who is high on the maintenance axis and give him or her the role of communicating with the team or getting the team together. If you are high on the maintenance axis but low on the performance axis, you can utilize a junior staff member who is good at detecting problems or creating strategies to raise the performance axis. Co-Leadership, with two or three people sharing the role, can be an effective solution.

Moreover, a person who is assigned to Co-Leadership will feel "I need to fulfill this part on behalf of the leader," so his motivation will increase. This can result in improved communication and team unity.

In addition, it will be a good experience for the junior staff member when he/she assumes leadership in the future. Thus, both the leader and the co-leaders benefit from Co-Leadership.

An example of Co-Leadership is the case of Mr. Rudy Giuliani, the mayor of New York at the time of 9/11 terrorist attacks. Mr. Giuliani has a great knowledge of leadership and has written several books about it. In his books, he says that a leader has strengths and weaknesses, and a key point in leadership is self-awareness because it will aid in creating a team, to further strengthen what one is good at and provide support in areas that need improvement. Mr. Giuliani's strengths are the ability to solve problems and the ability to take action in emergencies. Accordingly, he exercised leadership by taking the lead himself in taking action and enforcing the security of New York, especially in the aftermath of 9/11. But he was not good at developing person-to-person relationships for issues that require a long time to deal with, such as educational cases. Hence he utilized Co-Leadership by co-operating with others who did have skill in his weak areas.

Do you know and understand your strengths and weaknesses? Do you have any junior staff members or others who can support and help you strengthen your weaknesses? If possible, after you learn about your strengths and weaknesses, make a detailed action plan for how you can compensate for your weaknesses.

[6] The Path-Goal Theory

Changing the leadership type according to the members or environment

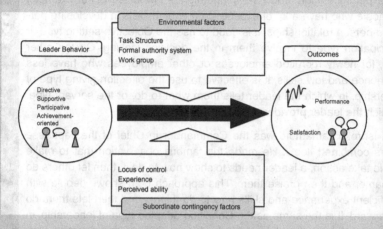

Figure 3.23. The Path-Goal theory

When you think about leadership, what style do you think is good?

For example, take a situation a leader decides everything on his own and gives directions to the members, such as "This needs to be taken care of this way," "You are not supposed to do it that way," and "Follow this schedule." Is it good to adopt a directive leadership behavior? Alternatively, is it good to have the "Support" type of leadership, in which members take the initiative and a leader provides support when problems occur? What about a participative leadership behavior, in which a leader says to the members, "What do you think about the vision of this project? Please participate in the decision making"? Or is it good to have an achievement-oriented leadership behavior, in which a leader sets an objective for the members, such as "The sales objective this year is X and the profit objective is Y. Please achieve those objectives," and "This project needs to be completed this way," and leave it to the members to achieve or complete them?

The fact is, there is no one absolute leadership style. The Path-Goal theory is a leadership theory that states that a leader's behavior is contingent upon the satisfaction, motivation, and performance of the subordinates. Then how do we use those leadership approaches according to the situation? There are two factors in deciding which one fits better.

The first factor concerns the team members. A person may have much or little experience, high or low skills, and high or low initiative. For example, for people who have a lot of experience and high skills in developing person-to-person relationships, it is good to use the Objective-setting type or Participation type to involve them in the decision-making. On the other hand, for newly recruited employees or other employees who have less experience and low skills, it is effective to use the direction-giving type of leadership, in which the leader tells them what to do, or the servant type, in which the leader provides support.

Adm. Isoroku Yamamoto was the Commander in Chief of the Japanese Navy's combined fleets. He made the famous observation that to make people take action, a leader needs to show how to do it, then let others do the same, and then praise them. This approach both shows people with insufficient experience and skills how to do things, and then lets them do it afterward. It is the same as the Condition-adapted type of leadership, in which you change the style of leadership, such as giving direction first, having them participate, and then giving support.

If you use the wrong leadership approach, such as using achievement-oriented leadership with people who do not have enough experience, they will naturally get confused, since they do not know what to do. Conversely, if you give directions for even simple tasks to people who have enough experience and skills, they will lose their motivation. Moreover, they will stop thinking, because all they need to do is follow the leader's directions all the time. This will inhibit their growth. Therefore, if you apply the wrong leadership, both the motivation and the skills of the members will not grow, and the team will not function well. Hence, to decide what kind of leadership is required, it is important to observe the members.

There are many cases in which a leader has a certain style that he or she is good at and keeps using that style all the time. For example, a leader uses the direction-giving type of leadership with any and all junior staff members because he/she did well using that approach in the past. Or things do not go well because a leader adopts an achievement-oriented leadership behavior with immature members because he/she has been doing well using that type so far.

Imagine a baseball player who is good at throwing straight balls. If he keeps throwing straight balls all the time just because he is good at it, eventually someone will hit the ball. A hitter who is good at hitting a straight ball will easily hit such a ball. Consequently, pitchers need to throw curves and splitters as well in order to get strikes and outs. Similarly, a leader needs to use leadership approaches effectively according to the situation. Generally, a leader tends to choose a style that he/she is good at. Nevertheless, it is important to apply these four styles according to the situation of the members.

Up to this point I have discussed choosing a leadership style that matches the members, but another factor is the business environment. The leadership style will change depending on the business environment.

An organization goes through various phases: the "initial" period when the business has just been started; the "growth" period, in which it develops and expands; the "mature" period, in which it has settled down to some extent; and the "change" period. In the initial period, in many cases, a leader needs to give strong leadership and the direction-giving type of leadership is relatively effective: "We are following this schedule for this matter." "We are doing it this way." "This needs to be taken care of this way." Advance the initiation and start-up rapidly with strong leadership. However, when a team gets bigger and has more people, a leader cannot give out all the directions. Also, if you continue to use a direction-giving type of leadership, junior staff members will wait for your orders and stop thinking on their own. In order to increase the motivation and skills of the members, the leadership style will need to be changed from the direction-giving type to the servant type, participation type, and objective-setting type as the company progresses from the growth period to the mature period. Then, in the change period, use directive leadership to make a big change, and then support the members by using the servant type. The type of leadership approach to be used depends on the members. If the skills, experience, and motivation of the members are high, you can use the participation type or objective-setting type leadership. Moreover, if you have someone who acts as a sub-leader, in order for you to decide which of the four leadership types you should employ, take note of what kind of leadership the sub-leader is using. By exercising these leadership styles effectively, you will be able to improve your performance and the members' satisfaction and motivation.

The key to the Path-Goal theory is to be aware of the different leadership styles available for use. Instead of continually using one style that you like, it is important to select an effective leadership style that fits the members and the business environment. In addition, if you have to adopt a style that you are not good at, you could use Co-Leadership. If you are not good at giving directions, you can employ Co-Leadership with a sub-leader who does have that skill. If you are not good at the servant style, you can work with a sub-leader who is good at it. Thus you will be able to exercise effective team leadership through Co-Leadership as well.

• Column ▼▼▼6

[7] Servant Leadership

Give the main role to the members in the Action phase

The leader takes the main role for directions (visions/strategies), and the members take the main role in the actual task/action phase.

Once the leader clarifies the vision, he/she gives effective support to the members to perform the actual tasks/actions. Then members will support customers effectively and lead the business to success.

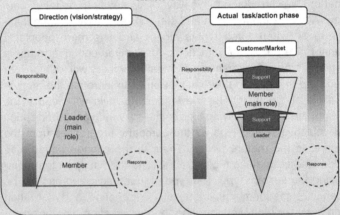

Figure 3.24.   Servant (support) type of leadership

(*Source*: Kenneth Blanchard)

• Column ▼▼▼7

This figure shows the servant (support) type of leadership, which is said to be an effective leadership approach used in companies in the West recently. To explain the servant type of leadership properly, here is a story. A group was traveling. One member did everything he was asked to do and solved any problems the others had, so everyone assumed that he was a servant for the group.

One day, this person was absent. Up to this point the group had had a smooth trip. But suddenly, because he was not there, they were at a loss as to where they needed to go, what they needed to do, and how they should solve immediate problems, As a result, the group could not continue fulfilling their objective, i.e. traveling. Then they finally realized that he was not a servant but a servant leader. They understood that he had been exercising leadership, creating visions, improving everyone's action skills, helping them grow, and supporting them through a servant-like approach.

The Action part of the Value model discussed earlier uses the servant type of leadership. In the Vision phase of creating visions, strategies, and values, a leader takes the main role and with it the responsibility to convey the visions to the members for them to follow. This is the case during the vision making stage, but in Servant Leadership, during the Action phase the members take the main role. For example, in the Action phase, in which a sales department expands its sales activities or a technology department starts designing and manufacturing, the leader–member relationship pyramid will change. Instead of the typical leader on top and members at the bottom, the leader will be at the bottom and the members, having taken on the main role, will be on top. The leader takes a supportive role to assist the members if mishaps occur and furnish whatever they lack. This is Servant Leadership. The advantage of Servant Leadership is a quicker response to customers. Members deal with the customers and the market and perform sales tasks directly. They can provide better service and products in addition to noticing problems.

Southwest Airlines, a US company, offers mainly domestic flights. It has put Servant Leadership into practice. One of the company's visions is to please their customers. Achievement of this vision is borne mainly by the cabin attendants, who provide services to please the passengers, according to the situation. For example, most airlines provide snacks to the passengers on their plane. In the case of Southwest Airlines, the cabin attendants may put on a little show of tossing bags of snacks to passengers, like playing catch. They may also hold a quiz or a game tournament and give out prizes to passengers. That is, the cabin attendants can decide how to carry out their services. The management team of Southwest Airlines determines the visions and directions, but the employees in the field take the main role of actually providing services to please customers and politely handling problems. These employees hold the authority and responsibility concerning the operations and services that they offer on the plane. Competition in the airline industry is very tough, and companies' performance in the industry generally is only fair. Nonetheless, Southwest

Airlines has been showing good management continuously, and its sales and profits have been increasing in the medium to long term.

The Ritz-Carlton Hotel chain gives its employees the authority to draw on the company budget up to a certain amount for things they think would benefit the customers in an emergency — without prior permission from the superiors. One day, a hotel guest checked out and left a document behind. A hotel staff member who found the document thought that it must be important, so he picked it up and jumped on an express train right away, without getting permission from his boss. He caught up with the hotel guest, who was heading to Tokyo, and handed him the document. It turned out that it was indeed a very important document, which the guest needed that day. Because of the hotel employee's independent action, the guest was very grateful. If the hotel employee had had to ask for prior permission from his boss, or some hotel rule had forbidden such action, the hotel guest would not have received his document in time and would have been in trouble at his company. In turn, this might have affected whether or not that company would use the hotel again. In this case, the grateful guest told others about this good service, and this led to increased business. This is an example in which the servant type of leadership functioned very well.

Shiseido also has been trying to spread Servant Leadership by giving more authority to salespeople and Shiseido Ladies so that they can take the main role in serving customers. CyberAgent, a company with many subsidiaries, allows managers in their 20s and 30s to manage the subsidiaries on their own. Naturally, the company provides them with support, but the point is that the parent company has benefited by leaving the actual business operations to leaders in the subsidiaries.

In the past, it was common for a leader to determine a vision and give direction to the members. But these days, the needs of customers change rapidly. In such a situation, you can respond to customers and the market quickly and appropriately if you let the members, who deal with the field directly, handle them by giving them some of the authority. In this way the servant type of leadership can be an effective leadership approach.

Now, we will consider how Servant Leadership will interact with the Path-Goal theory.

Naturally, members need to have experience, skill, and motivation in order to exercise leadership. Hence, a leader needs to cultivate members with those qualities and provide support to them to exercise good team leadership. Servant Leadership is a very effective approach if used appropriately.

To grow well you need a clear understanding of the strengths and weaknesses of the leader and those of the members, as well as the state of the business environment. Then, eventually, you want to shift to servant leadership. Do not forget: a leader needs to take the initiative to create visions and directions. Servant Leadership does not extend to showing where the company is going and what the company is doing. It is important to involve the members when you create a vision, but the leader needs to make the final decision and take the responsibility for it.

▼▼▼7 · Column

[8] Five-level hierarchy

Leadership that has both strength and humility

▼▼▼8 · Column

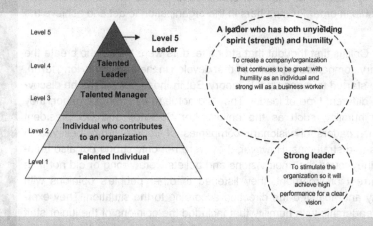

Figure 3.25. Five levels of leadership

Source: *Good to Great: Why Some Companies Make the Leap… and Others Do not by* James C. Collins)

This pyramid depicts a leadership model proposed in the best-selling book "*Good to Great: Why Some Companies Make the Leap… and Others Don't*" by James C. Collins (called "*Visionary Company 2*" in Japan, published by Nikkei BP). In his book, Mr. Collins notes a particular style of leadership that emerges at companies in their medium to long period of 10, 15 years or longer. He structured this into five levels of leadership.

The phases of leadership are as follows:

First, once a person joins a company and learns tasks, he/she needs to become a talented individual (Level 1: Highly Capable Individual).

Then, he/she works in a team with other people and produces good results as he/she works on team projects in addition to the individual tasks (Level 2: Individual Who Contributes to an Organization). In short, these correspond to "individual player" and "team player."

In Level 3 (Competent Manager), he/she manages and operates his/her own team. Generally, this is at the level of section chief or department manager.

Above that is the level of the Talented Leader and Management Executive (Level 4: Talented Leader).

Generally, leaders at this level create clear visions and exercise strong leadership in order for members in the organization to act and achieve the vision.

Author Collins first thought that strong leaders were those who create the visionary companies (companies that develop in the medium to long term), and he started to research this theory. But in those companies he discovered a different type of leader. They did not lead by strength; rather, they led by humility, such as the philosopher Socrates and US president Lincoln. Leaders of visionary companies of course firmly believed in visions and strategies. However, they were not only strong but also humble. If they found that their visions and beliefs were wrong or did not fit in the current environment, they listened to other people's opinions with humility and adjusted the direction according to the situation. They exercised leadership with humility that included the opinions of the junior staff members, co-workers, and customers. Moreover, most of the visionary companies are guided by Level 5 leaders, who have both strength and humility. Most people would assume that the strong leadership of Level 4 is the key, but Level 5 is above that; for an organization to develop and permanently endure, it is necessary to have leadership that has both strength and humility.

Let us look at some examples from the past. For example, Mr. Nakauchi of Daiei was a typical strong leader. At first, as its very strong leadership functioned well, Daiei expanded and grew. But it could not make changes when it needed to, and it had difficulty managing independently. Then it fell under the management of the Industrial Revitalization Corporation of Japan in

2005. Possible reasons for its troubles were that employees could not voice their opinions or submit suggestions when problems arose, or it may have been that leaders did not listen to the employees' opinions. Eventually, the management's visions became out of step with the times, and things went wrong.

One Level 5 leader who has both strength and humility is Mr. Soichiro Honda of Honda. He is not adept at accounting or financing, so he benefits from the skills of his business partner, Mr. Takeo Fujisawa, to manage Honda together. When he had a difference of opinion with a young engineer about an automobile, he discussed the matter thoroughly with the young man, engineer to engineer. The upshot was that Mr. Fujisawa backed down on his opinion and accepted that of the young engineer. This shows his humility, when even a company president can deal with employees in the field as equals and respect others' opinions.

Leaders can make companies and teams develop continuously by being strong and humble at the same time, by listening to the members' and others' ideas, and by correcting their own mistakes. The Level-5 Hierarchy is also a suggestion for exercising effective team leadership.

[9] Why is a starfish stronger than a spider?

There is a book "*The Starfish and the Spider: The Unstoppable Power of Leaderless Organizations*" by Ori Brafman and Rod A. Beckstrom. Starfish and spiders are somewhat similar in shape. For example, if you divide them in half, a spider will die but a starfish will survive because it has a strong life force in which each separated piece can regenerate itself. To put it simply, this book says that organizations will develop better when the powers are distributed, similar to a starfish, rather than having all the powers in one place, like the head of a spider. In the past, organizations had all the powers in one place, but nowadays, organizations with distributed powers are functioning well. Similarly, these authors predict that organizations and leaderships of the future will resemble a starfish, in which the powers and functions are distributed. This is similar to the "all-member leadership" that I propose, in which everyone shares the same vision and takes the initiative to exercise leadership to lead to improve themselves, their team, the world, and society.

[10] What is Remote Leadership?

(Leadership for members at distant locations)

Compared to Japan, the United States is a vast country. In the US, owing to recent developments in communications technology, teleworking or telecommuting has become widespread. According to research conducted in the United States by the Society of Human Resource Management in 2007, about 48% of companies in the US offer their employees one day or more of telecommuting a week. The number of companies that offer telecommuting is increasing among large, small, and medium-sized companies. The pioneer in telecommuting is AT&T, a communications company; in which approximately half of its employees work from home. Here is an example of one California businessman. He is a manager of a company that is located in Minnesota — a 4- to 5-hour flight — and all of his junior staff members live in the Midwest and on the East Coast. Thus he sees the members only a few times a year when they have a company conference. Nonetheless, he does his job by staying at home and communicating with members using telephone conferences and e-mails. Companies can cut back on office rent and commuting allowances (gas and ticket money). Employees can use their time more effectively because they do not have to spend time commuting or they can live anywhere they choose. It would seem that telecommuting holds advantages for both the companies and the employees. On the downside, some problems do exist, such as leaders having difficulty keeping the members motivated, since they do not normally see each other in person. In the United States, the exercising of leadership of the team and junior staff members whom you do not see often is called "Remote Leadership." This Remote Leadership will be required not only in the United States but also in Japan in the future.

Due to improvements in IT technology, we increasingly see the sales approach of calling on customers directly from home and returning home directly when work is done, or the free-address system style of office, in which employees come and go during work and are not assigned individual desks. For example, sales people visit their customers and report to the company by cell phone or e-mail from outside or home. They rarely need to go in to the company office. More companies are adopting this style these days. (There are also other reasons, such as cases in which outlying offices are closed due to company consolidation and the remaining offices are only in big cities.) Systems engineers and consultants of IT companies in particular use desks assigned to them at the customer's office all the time and thus do not need to go in to the company they actually belong to. In some cases, the boss and the team members work at different locations. Such cases are not so rare these days.

In the last 10 years, working in a remote environment — in which a boss and junior staff members or co-workers do not see each other while they are working — is increasing dramatically in Japan. It has made business operations more efficient. But that does not mean that it has made things easier.

A survey at multiple Japanese and foreign-affiliated companies found common problems for employees working in a remote environment.

Problems of junior staff members

The increased efficiency enabled by the introduction of IT has generated more work to do and less intellectual challenge. They feel isolated because they do not get together much with their co-workers and boss.

There is little opportunity for young workers to learn about their work and experience on-the-job training from senior staff members and bosses.

Their motivation does not increase because they receive one-way directions and information from the head office or boss.

Problems of bosses

It is difficult to manage the team because they do not see their junior staff members often. Discrepancies arise because the bosses' intention cannot be passed along clearly to the junior staff members. They have to cultivate and evaluate junior staff members whom they seldom meet.

The increased efficiency enabled by the introduction of IT has generated more work to do and there is no time left over for cultivating the junior staff members.

How does a leader exercise Remote Leadership to solve these problems?

To exercise Remote Leadership, a leader needs to focus on three things. We call this the Remote Leadership 3E Model, and present the practice approach at seminars for companies.

Remote Leadership 3E Model

Engagement: To build a trust relationship with the other person.
Empowerment: To support the other person in order to be able to delegate tasks to him or her.

• Column ▼▼▼10

Evaluation: To give evaluations and feedback.
Specifically, the key to the success of Remote Leadership is Engagement.

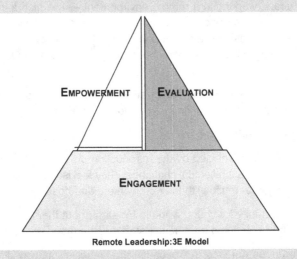

Remote Leadership:3E Model

Figure 3.26. Remote Leadership: 3E model

Dr. Albert Mehrabian, a US psychologist, has conducted experiments that show the impact of communication on people. He found that 7% is verbal information, such as the contents of a story; 38% is vocal information, such as the speaking speed and tone; and 55% is visual information, such as body language and appearance. In short, in a remote environment, you can convey only 7% of your intention to the other person through e-mails, and only 45% by including telephonic conversation (7% + 38%). Communication in a remote environment is ineffective when compared with face-to-face communication. Thus it is important to have many opportunities to communicate with the other person, even if just by telephone or e-mails, in order to build a trust relationship. Moreover, in addition to having more opportunities to communicate, it is important to make each communication as positive as possible. If the communication is between a boss and junior staff members, sometimes a boss will need to give them stern feedback. This is especially hard to endure in a remote environment. If you give feedback in the absence of a trust relationship, the other person may not accept it or may react adversely.

In the future, more business operations will be conducted in remote environments in Japan. Organizations will be more active if more and more business people become more conscious about Remote Leadership and practice it. As a result, it will affect the achievements of business itself.

• Column ▼▼▼10

➤ CHAPTER 4 ◄

GLOBAL LEADERSHIP

1. What is Global Leadership? (WHAT)

— Take a world view, see the world as a stage, and take action

Now that I have discussed Self-Leadership (leading yourself) and Team Leadership (leading a team), I would like you to think about the world that we live in today. In essence, the three waves of change — internetization, globalization and diversification — have brought about a globalized world that is vastly different from what it used to be in the past. As a result, an important form of leadership is required: Global Leadership. Global Leadership is the ability to combine various leadership styles with an understanding of the world to lead a team consisting of members from differing cultures. This chapter explains the necessity of Global Leadership and how these leadership styles can be applied in reality.

2. Why is Global Leadership Needed? (WHY)

In August 2007 I had the opportunity to participate in a discussion with business school students of the Indian Institute of Technology in New Delhi.

About 70% of Indian companies' business at that time was with the West. One of the members in our group asked them, "Between the Western countries, the Asian countries and places in India, where would India most want to expand business in the future?"

We were expecting them to answer that they would want India to do more business with Asia or Japan. But the question seemed to perplex them. To them, it did not matter whether it was the United States, Europe, or Asia. They do not think about which country to do business with, rather, they think about the world as a whole. They just find whatever venue is best for their business, regardless of national borders or differences between countries. This way of thinking, in which the world is viewed as a whole, was very new to us Japanese visitors, and the concept stimulated our imagination in a new direction.

Japanese people tend to group the markets into four categories: the domestic market within Japan, the Asian market, the European market, and the market in the United States. But people in India do not think that way. Their ability to see the world as they do is one of the elements that is helping India to succeed and grow in the global market. The fact is that the Indians already possess a global sense and global strategies. I believe we have to improve on cultivating a global sense in our own leadership.

As mentioned earlier, the Internet is transforming the world into one global entity. (As of 2007, the number of people using the Internet amounted to over 700 million. That is approximately 10% of the total world population.) The information sources, suppliers of products and services, and selling markets are also merging. As a result, you will be able to exercise more effective leadership when you think of the world as a whole instead of dividing it into markets.

I visited Shanghai, China in January 2008. Sprucing up for the upcoming Beijing Olympics in August 2008 and the Shanghai Expo in 2010, the Chinese had constructed a row of strikingly modern tall buildings housing high-class hotels and offices, brought in more luxury cars from the West and Japan, and put the world's first linear-motor rail car into operation. These enhancements of the hardware side are emblematic of the world today.

They still have problems on the software side, such as in the service sector, but I sensed in the people a strong vitality and that they hope and expect China to attain outstanding growth and affluence.

The BRICs Report, named after the initial letters of the countries it covers — Brazil, Russia, India, and China — predicts the development of these countries and mentions that Russia and Brazil similarly have been developing rapidly.

Also, along with BRIC, there is no doubt that the countries referred to as the Next Eleven (or N-11) — Bangladesh, Egypt, Indonesia, Iran, Mexico, Nigeria, Pakistan, the Philippines, South Korea, Turkey, and Vietnam — will also enjoy rapid and substantial economic growth due to internetization and globalization.

Today, countries are having ever greater effect on each other in various aspects. For example, if there is a conflict in one area and its oil production goes down, the price of oil will suddenly rise throughout the world. If one area is experiencing a good economy, this will affect the world economy as procurement and sales increase there.

As people in developing countries gain skills, it becomes possible for them to participate in the same kinds of business as people in developed countries. Jobs such as marketing call-center operators and IT and other customer-service assistants can be outsourced to developing countries via the Internet to take advantage of the lower pay rate — half, a third, a fifth or even, in some cases, a tenth that of that in a developed country. As a result, a rising number of people in the United States are losing these jobs to English speakers in developing countries, such as India. This is a very serious issue in the United States these days.

As the Japanese language is unique to Japan, this phenomenon is less of a problem there. Nevertheless, there are some cases in which Japanese companies are outsourcing telephone operations and computer programming to Dalian in China, New Delhi in India, or Vietnam. This flow will accelerate and is unlikely to stop.

Looking at it another way, India, China, and East Europe are accepting business from developed countries proactively. If you continue to focus only on smaller areas or countries, you will not be able to perceive the overall flow of world business. As a result, you may be hit by some unforeseen business loss.

As a familiar example, let us consider a neighborhood coffee shop.

This coffee shop's rivals used to be just the coffee shops and cafés or restaurants in the immediate vicinity. But today, its competitors also include Starbucks and Tully's from overseas; recently even McDonald's has also entered the "coffee boutique" business. If you think that you do not need to worry about the world, as you are just doing your business in a local area without keeping an eye on global trends, there is a risk that you may meet with trouble in managing your business.

It is necessary not only for management executives but also for leaders, managers, employees in the field, and part-time workers to take a wide-screen view of the world and exercise leadership according to each person's role.

In contrast, if you catch and ride the waves of world trends well, even a small store can expand into the world. For example, Yoshinoya, of beef bowl fame, and Watami, a Japanese-style bar, have already extended their store chains into Europe and Asia proactively.

With the positive and negative effects of globalization, we should apply a form of leadership that can help us extract the benefits and make the best of the changing circumstances in globalization.

For example, it is well known that small- and medium-sized factories that have a distinctly high technology level are concentrated in Tokyo's Ota ward and the Higashi Osaka area in Osaka. These areas used to manufacture products for companies in Japan. But these days, with the markets of the world becoming one, they have extended their high-tech products to the West and Asia.

Boeing in the United States and Airbus in Europe buy parts from small- and medium-sized Japanese enterprises to be used as important components in the world's most advanced aircraft. Additional examples are cases in which advanced technologies of small- and medium-sized enterprises are used for innovative medical equipment. These days, even small companies or factories in a small corner of Japan can enjoy great success in the world.

In London, I have a business partner referred to here as Ms S. She can handle business matters in Japanese and English.

She understands my business very well. Ms. S and her friend, a native English speaker, also have the know-how to make proper project proposals in English for foreign-affiliated companies. Thus I can "outsource globally" to Ms. S.

For example, if I finish a meeting with a customer at 6:00 p.m. in Japan, to prepare a project proposal for speedy delivery to the customer, I would normally have to either work overtime that night or start early the next day.

However, due to the nine-hour time difference (6:00 p.m. Japan time is 9:00 a.m. of the same day in Great Britain) and global outsourcing, when I inform Ms. S, via the Internet, of the content of the meeting with the customer, the customer's needs, and the big picture of the project proposal, she will work on it from 9:00 a.m. to 6:00 p.m. in her timezone.

Creating more opportunities as suppliers and markets open up worldwide. Creating more opportunities by making use of the time differences 24/7.	Competitors are not just domestic companies but companies all over the world. Becomes very busy, as business goes on 24/7. Requires language skills (e.g., English, Chinese).

Figure 4.1. Advantages and disadvantages of globalization (environment)

Since 6:00 p.m. in Great Britain is 3:00 a.m. the next day in Japan, the project proposal for the customer is ready by 9:00 a.m. Japan time, and I can give the proposal to the customer right away.

My customers often say, "You must have been up very late! Did you work all night?" No, that night I spent my time having dinner, relaxing with customers, family, or friends. And I got enough sleep, too.

This sort of quick turnaround is possible thanks to world outsourcing, making use of the time difference and the Internet.

Globalization has its disadvantages as well as advantages. That notwithstanding, the paradigm shift toward globalization will never stop. Rather, it will accelerate rapidly in the future. A paradigm shift in which people can find advantages will never stop. If you understand the world and how it is connected, you can make your business, as well as your private life, truly interesting and effective, by making good use of the various resources in the world.

Consequently, you will need to understand the advantages and disadvantages of globalization. Also, you will also need to understand your own and your team's strengths and weaknesses in using globalization. Then you can practice the strategies and actions that maximize the strengths and minimize the weaknesses.

How do we do this? I will explain in the next section.

3. How Do We Put Global Leadership into Practice? (HOW)

3.1. *Synergize global and local leadership*

— View things globally, and practice and take action locally

In Global Leadership, it is important to have a local point of view, in which you consider your own area and field, in addition to a global point of view.

While you look at the world and seek out the best practices, you need to cover the local areas in that field.

For example, the American chain store Walmart is trying to expand their business in Japan by working with Seiyu — though that does not seem to be working that well so far. The reason behind this seems to be that Walmart is focusing more on going global than on paying attention to the local aspects, such as providing products and services that suit consumers in Japan. In globalization it is important to see both the global and the local picture.

In terms of the synergies between both global and local needs, in addition to the products and services, you can say the same about the people in companies and organizations. It seems to be a better idea to use local personnel to take action, according to global management visions and strategies. Foreign-affiliated companies hire local people for management who understand the global visions and strategies well, instead of sending over all of the executive officers from the home country. By doing so, they can exercise effective leadership with a good balance of the global and local.

Global Leadership is leadership that includes both the global and the local levels of leadership and uses them well. In fact, if this enhances progress, whether one is in the local or the head office would not make much difference in the organization. General Electric (GE) is an organization that forms its teams based on the abilities, skills, and experience of their personnel, no matter what countries they are from.

3.2. *Accept each other's differences*

Of course, people from the same country have differences as well, but the point is that different countries have different national characters, histories, cultures, religions, and customs.

It is important to understand the culture of another country. For example, Japanese people have a stronger group-consciousness than American people. When companies from overseas start a business in Japan, they have to exercise leadership that appreciates group dynamics.

Conversely, if a Japanese company expands its business to the United States, they need to understand and respect the strong individualism of Americans. They will have to create a framework that allows for individual talents to flourish while ensuring teamwork, in order to improve communication and work toward a common objective.

Japanese people are earnest and are very punctual. In comparison, if you work with people in China or India, they often do not arrive on time or do not finish their tasks on time. They are not sorry about this development. It is necessary to adjust your business practices by understanding those cultural differences in order to properly make suitable rules, execute contracts, or advance time schedules.

Moreover, people in Japan hold seniority in high esteem and consider it natural to respect elders and superiors. However, many countries do not practice this. In the West, people place more emphasis on actual ability and position rather than age. If you try to lead people without understanding such differences, you may get a bad reaction from them.

As a leader, it is important to understand the differences and benefit from them rather than holding back because of cultural differences. It is best if you can adopt the best practices in the differing business cultures and use them well by accepting other people's ways in addition to your own.

Understanding this basic element is essential in practicing Global Leadership.

3.3. *Deal with each other while sharing the same perspective (as human beings)*

Recently, I talked with Mr. N of Kagome and Mr. T of Toshiba Machine, who work in Shanghai, China, and asked them about the characteristics of successful leaders overseas.

They told me the following.

If a leader discriminates (e.g., "Japanese people are…, Chinese people are…, Western people are…"),

→ people will dislike him → he will fail.

If a leader does *not* discriminate (i.e., is a person who can deal anyone as an equal human being)

→ people will like him → he will succeed.

In addition, Mr. A, a former president in Taiwan for Takeda Pharmaceutical Company, says, "Some bad things about Japanese leaders are that they tend to think of Western people as superior to them and Asian people as inferior to them. This will cause foreigners to dislike them. The key is to deal with anyone as an equal human being, from the same perspective, regardless of whether they are from the West, Asia, or anywhere else."

The point is, even though there are differences, as mentioned earlier, you must see people as equal human beings and deal with them in a straightforward manner, instead of seeing them as higher or lower.

▶ Three elements for cultivating the global human resource

• Column ▼▼▼11

Due to the development of the Internet and the global economy, the world is fast becoming one and business activities are increasingly becoming borderless. Business involving Japanese companies is rapidly changing, evolving away from the traditional model, in which they manufacture products in Japan and import them, to manufacturing products in each country and expanding their business there.

Along with such changes, the type of personnel required is changing as well. Recently I have been encountering many cases in which domestic sales experts or manufacturing experts, regardless of whether they have prior overseas experience, are suddenly sent to offices overseas as experts.

Moreover, it is not uncommon for junior staff members or even bosses in Japan to be foreigners, even at a traditional Japanese company. This is because of mergers with and acquisitions of foreign-affiliated companies or, in some instances, direct hiring of foreigners.

How do we exercise leadership to respond to such changes?

When you think of the elements of the global human resource, you can see that three elements are required, as follows.

(1) Language skill
(2) Management skill
(3) Global perspective

Language skill is, of course, a primary element required for communication. It is not necessary to be fluent but it is more important to have the feeling that you want to tell something to others and that you want to understand about others.

As for management skill, it is necessary to know the basics of the main subjects you learn at Masters in Business Administration (MBA) programs, such as strategies, marketing, and finance. When you are doing business overseas, you will realize that there are many business people who have studied business administration. As you have to do business with them with a shared perspective, the knowledge and framework of MBA programs can be said to be the general knowledge in global business.

Third is the global perspective or global mind. I stayed in Hong Kong for business for five years, and from my own experience, this element is crucial. Even if you are fluent in other languages and have knowledge of management, exercising leadership or conducting business in the global environment will not be easy if you cannot understand or accept a different culture.

To exercise Global Leadership, you must improve your leadership by having those three elements as a foundation. But you cannot learn any of these in a short period. If you want to exercise leadership in global business, you will need to enlighten yourself in the medium to long term.

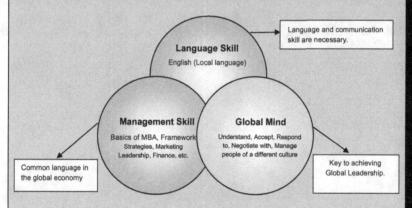

Figure 4.2.   Three elements for cultivating the global human resource

➤ CHAPTER 5 ◀

SOCIAL LEADERSHIP

1. What is Social Leadership? (WHAT)

Social Leadership is about understanding the country or society that you belong to and leading it. Here, "society" includes not only human society but also the global environment and living creatures other than human beings. This is because if we damage the environment such that animals and plants cannot live, human beings cannot survive either.

A leader's perspective must have a long time-line, encompassing the medium to long term, as well as a basic understanding of historical lessons in relation to our society and the global environment.

These qualities will increase your capacity as a leader and make it easier for others to accept you as a leader, including your viewpoints on human beings, the world, and history. This is good not only for yourself but also for your team, society, and the world.

2. Why is Social Leadership Needed?

In today's society, individuals think only about themselves and companies think only about their own interests. It seems that we are lacking a social point of view for thinking about other individuals and societies. Some people think about what they can do about societal situations and the global environment at the level of the individual, and some companies take some action on environment issues. Even so, *all* individuals and teams (including companies) are members of the overarching human society, so we all need to think more about society and take action on its behalf.

Many companies these days tend to focus more on pursuing sales and profit and returns for the shareholders. Of course it is necessary to pursue such things in order for a company to keep going; but if they do only that, they will become just an economic machine.

In the 21st century, companies and organizations in a human society become socially responsible only when they pursue both profitability and social goals in a good balance instead of just pursuing only their own profit. It is essential for companies and leaders to consider their connection with society — not only for the sake of society as whole, but also for the sake of themselves and their teams.

For example, if oil companies keep exploiting a large amount of the limited oil resources on the earth, the world's oil resources will eventually be depleted. As a result, oil companies will lose business. Moreover, if seafood processing companies, which catch, process, and sell seafood, catch more than necessary for their own profit, the oceans will have no resources left, and the company will not be able to manage its business. In fact, due to overexploitation, certain sea animals are already becoming scarce.

We live in an era of mass production and mass consumption designed to make life easier for human beings.

According to statistics, the earth's population has been increasing rapidly, reaching 1 billion in 1800, 2 billion in 1900, 3 billion in 1960, 4 billion in 1974, 5 billion in 1987, 6 billion in 1999, and 6.6 billion in 2007. If this trend continues, it is predicted that the earth may hold over 9 billion people in 2050.

In such a situation, what will happen if we maintain the current rate of mass production and mass consumption? The earth's resources will be plundered, and the world will be littered with industrial waste and public trash. The world's economy, industry, and even life on earth itself may not be sustainable. The same can be said of the oil and automobile industries. In addition, there is a possibility that this will result in a crisis not only to the economy and industry but also to the very existence of the human race.

The earth belongs not just for the people who live on it at present. It also belongs to our ancestors and future descendants. If we regard the earth as belonging just to the people who are alive now, we can only leave to future generations an earth and a society with an environment that is destroyed by industrial waste, is full of social problems, and can no longer continue to grow.

Then again, there are some companies and leaders who take the global environment, society, and the future of humanity into account. They are now putting forth efforts to protect global resources and employ and protect the weak.

Take the example of Toyota and hybrid cars, which can run using either gasoline or electrical energy. Toyota spent a huge sum of money on the initial investment in developing them and is now continuing their development and sale. With such a large outlay expended for the startup, it took a very long time for Toyota to recoup its investment in the hybrid car market. Nonetheless, Toyota is acting in consideration of the global environment and the future of the entire automobile industry.

As a result of such efforts, people in the world are more conscious about protecting the global environment, and more consumers are more conscious about society, choosing Toyota's hybrid cars even if the price is higher than regular gasoline cars. This has turned out to be good business for Toyota.

This not only produces a good result for the company (team) but also builds motivation in team members, who can take pride in knowing that are developing, manufacturing, and selling earth-friendly hybrid cars.

Aeon, a general merchandise store, carries out earth-friendly ideas such as reducing the use of plastic shopping bags by using reusable shopping baskets and planting young trees to counteract desertification caused by human activities.

These activities are indeed evidence of respectable leadership.

If you exercise leadership like that, the company or organization will gain trust and respect from the consumers and the public at large. As a result, people will purchase the products and services of that company or organization. This will bring the sales achievement and profit for the company in the end.

From the era of strong leadership to the era of *strength + kindness + correctness = respectable leadership*

If Self-Leadership and Team Leadership are improved, individuals and teams will become strong. In Global Leadership, however, the scope is wider; in addition to thinking about yourself, you will have to consider society and the world in order to take action.

Of course, it is necessary to think about yourself and your team. But at the same time, you will need to look at the big picture, that is, think about society and the world in order to think and take well-considered action. This is one of the wonderful things about human beings — the fact that, unlike other animals, we can contemplate such issues.

One of the management principles at Panasonic is "Co-existence and Co-prosperity." This is precisely about existing and flourishing together with society and the world — including customers, clients, and others — rather than thinking solely about ourselves.

Newly recruited Panasonic employees will learn this principal of Co-existence and Co-prosperity. That will help them to be proud and responsible, rather than inconsiderate about interests outside the company and solely bent on gaining more profit and salary for themselves. They will understand that their jobs and activities are for the benefit of their customers and society in general.

Social Leadership — leadership that considers society — will result in developing one's own strengths and goodness as well as one's own happiness and satisfaction.

Recently many companies have told me, "The motivation of the team members and leaders is getting low," and "We want to raise the employees' motivation."

Employee motivation is a significant issue for many companies and teams.

The things of value being provided to the society by individuals or teams are connected to the fundamental desires of human beings. Basically, most people want to have a better society and be a useful person in it. Few truly want to harm society.

As examples, people's motivation will improve if they know that their jobs or their products and services make customers' lives easier, improve the quality of life, support disadvantaged people through donations, or contribute to the improvement of the global environment.

These social activities can only increase people's motivation.

A certain medium-sized company plants young trees in a desert, commensurate with their profit.

They share openly with the employees how much company profit has increased and how many trees they have planted. By the company actions, employees can increase their motivation — feeling that they will be able to plant another young tree in the desert if they push themselves to try a little bit harder, even if they are tired that day.

This is an example in which a social activity is affecting the team members' motivation. In Social Leadership, working not only for themselves but also to contribute to others and society can be one of the elements for improving the members' motivation.

From now on, rather than individuals and teams that are merely strong, it is that the kind and respectful individuals who will be in demand. Author Raymond Chandler says in one of his novels, "People cannot live if they are not strong. People are meaningless if they are not kind." I totally agree. Individuals and teams cannot live if they are not strong. If they are not kind, they are meaningless. Social Leadership is leadership that possesses both strength and kindness.

3. How Do We Put Social Leadership into Practice? (HOW)

Then how do we put Social Leadership into practice?

First, it is vital to realize again that you and your team, and society and the world, are involved with and affect each other. You need to understand that any of your actions, or your team's actions, affect society, and be able to see that relationship and connection.

For example, when a pharmaceutical company releases a new medicine, it can save many peoples' lives and reduce suffering from sickness. Even if you are just the person in charge of developing a product, a medicine cannot be developed without you. Even if you are just one of the sales team, without you, hospitals or patients cannot receive information about the characteristics and effectiveness of the product itself. Everyone involved shares an important role in saving people's lives and reducing the suffering of sickness.

Naturally, companies cannot exist without gaining profits, and individuals cannot live without earnings. Those are necessary in our life.

Some people work with an attitude of "I'am developing this product just because I have to do it for the company," or "I'am doing sales activities to increase sales just to meet my assigned quota," or "I'am working just to put food on the table." Instead, you will be able to have more pride and confidence in your job by thinking about the significance of your work, such as how it contributes to the team, customers, society, and the world.

A social leader needs to understand that he himself must take action and share the significance of the work with the team members.

As I stressed in Chapter 3 regarding Team Leadership, doing so will improve the team's motivation, skills, and ability to get things done.

For example, someone who deals with human resource education will be able to create a better society or future by conducting better personnel training to cultivate better people.

Likewise, exercising Social Leadership involves contemplating, sensing, and expanding the circle that includes the relationship of you with your team, and of your team with society and the world.

Imagine a circle. A person's individual arc is a part of a circle. It is impossible to make a circle with just one arc, and the circle cannot be perfect if any of its parts are missing.

Picture yourself as a part of the circle that affects society. If you try to draw a circle by yourself, it will be a tiny one. But if you cooperate with many other people, it will be a bigger circle and have a bigger effect on society.

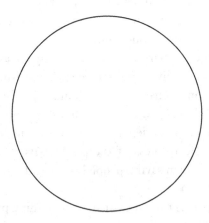

It is an unfortunate fact that some business and social activities seem to have a negative effect on society. For example, when an automaker manufactures a car, they need to use steel, oil, and many other materials. In terms of diminishing global resources, this has a negative effect on society.

Nonetheless, a consumer who buys this car can enrich his life by putting the car to good use. Also, such a product can help facilitate business and create social value. Moreover, this will generate wages for the daily lives of the automaker's employees and bring profits to the suppliers of car parts and raw materials and their employees. In addition, the profits that those companies make will become the basis for funding social services through national or local taxes.

Thus, when you look at things in the big picture instead of looking at them individually, if they have more positive effects than negative effects, the business itself is positive and should continue and advance. Any social or economic activities have both positive and negative sides. To consider things in the big picture, we need to look at both sides rather than just one.

I used to feel that there were too many negative aspects for society to justify consumer electronics makers' making electronic products in large volumes. I considered this an era in which there were already too many such instances in Japan.

But then again, today I look at countries that have a low standard of living, in which televisions, refrigerators, and cars are not yet available nationwide. I now realize that such products definitely have some positive aspects. Products like these can save much time and enrich people's lives in those countries, just as they have done in the West and Japan in the past.

I have learned that a judgment should be made comprehensively, by looking at things from both sides, viewing the big picture and seeking a good balance between elements.

If you want to create a company that continues to succeed and grow, you need to achieve a good balance between the needs of society and those of profit in the short term. If you do something that is harmful to society, you may suffer a great loss later on.

For example, consider Snow Brand Milk (Hokkaido's famous dairy company), which caused great problems by selling products that were past their expiration date. They made a profit in the short term, but their anti-societal activities were revealed by a whistle-blower later on. As a result, the incidents had a dramatic effect on the very existence of those companies.

There have been more such cases recently. In the 20th century, when the Internet was far less widespread, in-house or proprietary information was out of reach to outsiders. Such information was not as open to the public as it now is in the 21st century. In contrast, in this era of interneti-zation, anyone, even an employee in the field or a part-time worker, can easily obtain and release information via the Internet.

Anti-societal activities that were kept in the dark in the past are gradu-ally being brought to light. Society is becoming more transparent, and anti-societal or inhumane activities are quickly becoming revealed to the public.

In such a business environment, it is necessary for the leadership to have "correctness," which is the foundation of Social Leadership.

As another example, there was a company that used to bury industrial waste in the ground in a certain area, which was not forbidden by law at that time. This became a big social issue, in that this practice would bring about an adverse effect on the global environment, and the company's image declined greatly.

Social Leadership does not take any action that is considered to be "incorrect" — or have the possibility of being incorrect — toward the wel-fare of society, human beings, or the global environment, even if such actions are not yet forbidden by law. Such correct conduct will bring con-tinuous success and growth to a company as a result.

Some social activities may have aspects that are negative at one point in time, yet can be positive in the medium to long term.

Social Leadership involves taking action by looking at things three, five, 10, and perhaps 20, 30, and 50 years ahead, rather than just pursuing a short profits each time.

Recently, many teams and leaders are increasingly engaging proactively in activities to benefit society.

For example, take the 1% Club of the Japan Business Federation (Nippon Keidanren). This club is a group of companies and individuals who strive to use 1% or more of their ordinary profit or disposable income, or 1% or more of their time, for social action programs. If companies and individuals take part in such a group, they gain social respect, and con-sumers may feel that they want to purchase the products or services of such companies. As a result, there will be profit in the long term for the teams that engage in such activities.

Such activities will increase more and more in the future, as consider-ation grows toward the global environment and society.

The correct behavior of individuals and teams will be connected to other elements of the TO BE model — strength and kindness — and this will bring continuing success and growth to individuals and teams.

Thus, you will be able to improve Social Leadership by understanding the connection between you or your team and society and by thinking and taking actions that will be positive for society as a whole, even if it is but a little step forward.

▶ Essentially, people want to do the right thing

• • •

In my experience with meeting so many people in human resource cultivation seminars at companies and universities for business as well as privately, I have never met anyone who wanted to do bad things or harm society initially. No one that I have ever met wanted to destroy society or hurt someone.

When I ask people at seminars what kind of person they want to be or what kind of team they want to build, most of them tell me that they want to be a person who is fun to be with, kind, and full-hearted, and that they want to create a team that achieves a vision to make society better and learns from each other and enjoys business together.

This means that it is vital to exercise leadership that improves and makes use of those good aspects that people naturally have.

Essentially, human beings want to do the right thing. An important element of Social Leadership is that a leader must get the members to do socially right things and guide them to social awareness and action through dialogues or coaching. A leader needs to foster an environment where members can express ideas and opinions easily.

Mr. Matsushita, the founder of Panasonic, did not feel "We do not need to think about society. Let's just beat out the competition and make as much profit as we can." If he had, the thousands of employees of Panasonic's subsidiaries worldwide would not have followed him. Customers would have stopped purchasing products from such a company or leader, and as a result, the company would not have become one that achieves trillions of yen in annual sales.

Mr. Matsushita had a strong belief in creating an abundant social life in society through business activities. He said, "Let us enrich society by

• Column ▶▼▼12

spreading good electronics products throughout the world." He made this the management philosophy and conveyed it to all employees. He exercised Social Leadership aimed at making the entire society affluent by making people's lives more convenient so they could have more free time. That is why Panasonic has become a big organization and is esteemed by its customers and society.

Sony too has a company philosophy that aims to bring about world affluence by developing innovative products that the world has never seen before. They aim to have leadership that makes the company grow and develop continuously for a long time instead of just for the short term.

To some extent, masters of leadership posses a social element, whether they are the heads of companies, leaders or managers, or employees in the field. This means that not only the management executives of major companies but also leaders, managers, or field employees will be able to improve their skills to be a master of leadership by adopting such a point of view.

Regardless of the position they are in, people who can lead themselves or teams mindful of society and the world, and create something of value, are all World Class Leaders.

Donating a part of your income to society or contributing some of your free time for the improvement of your local community and its people, and participating in constructive activities for the environment, such as protecting natural resources, are all examples of respect-worthy World-Class Leadership.

Profit has its place, but people should also pursue good causes that have social value.

A leader becomes respectable as a result of exercising leadership that takes social aspects into consideration. This is done by improving the solidarity of the team and the motivation of the members in order to lead their business to success.

• Column ▼▼▼12

▶ CHAPTER 6 ◀

CONCLUSION

1. All Leadership Approaches are Connected

In this book, World-Class Leadership, so far I have discussed Self-Leadership (Chapter 2), Team Leadership (Chapter 3), Global Leadership (Chapter 4), and Social Leadership (Chapter 5). These four approaches to leadership are inseparable.

Through exercising Self-Leadership to understand and lead yourself, you all be able to exercise Team Leadership to lead a team.

When you lead a team, you will exercise Team Leadership more effectively after you have a good understanding of yourself, the world, and society. Exercising Global and Social Leadership to understand and lead globally and within society leads to Self Leadership and Team-Leadership, in a cycle.

These four leadership styles — Self-, Team, Global, and Social Leadership — are interlinked and do not stand alone.

Moreover, also interacting and connecting with each other are the Three Actions model of leadership (Vision, Action, and Learning) and the Ways-of-Being model of leadership — Strength, Kindness, Fun, and Correctness — which are used together to exercise better leadership.

2. To the Next Era

In this book, I have discussed leadership that corresponds to the internetization, globalization, and diversification that have burgeoned in the 21st century.

The leadership approach should always be suited to the particular environment. There is no particular leadership approach that you can apply in every environment and era.

It is necessary to exercise leadership that fits the social environment at all times. Accordingly, when society or the environment changes, we need to apply different types of leadership.

Up to this point I have talked about ways of thinking for leadership that correspond to societal and business environments. But as those environments change further, we need to come up with a new type of leadership that corresponds to the new social and business environment.

I believe that in any era, exercising leadership that fits the era will lead to the success and growth of people and organizations and the happiness of all people.

In conclusion, I would like to emphasize that in and after the 21st century, everyone must step up and take a main role by exercising leadership according to his position, instead of only certain people, such as heads or executives of an organization, taking leadership. This will be beneficial for individuals, teams, and the world toward creating a better future.